Do the Windows Open?

JULIE HECHT

DO THE
WINDOWS
OPEN?

RANDOM HOUSE

NEW YORK

All of the stories that appear in this collection were
originally published, in somewhat different form, in *The New Yorker.*

Library of Congress Cataloging-in-Publication Data
Hecht, Julie.
Do the windows open? / Julie Hecht.
p.   cm.
ISBN 0-679-45201-X
I. Title.
PS3558.E29D6   1997
813'.54—dc20   96-33139

Random House website address: http://www.randomhouse.com/

Printed in the United States of America on acid-free paper

24689753

First Edition

In memory of my father and mother,
David Hecht and Eva Shan

CONTENTS

Do the Windows Open?

Perfect Vision

December 21

Dear Elizabeth,

Although we haven't spoken in more than a year (I believe it was before last Christmas when you stopped calling me and refused to tell me why), I feel I should warn you about Mr. Kropstadt, the German, or the Kraut, as we used to call him—the man who owns Osborn's Opticians, on Park Avenue. I was there last December, about a year ago, and his behavior and demeanor convinced me that he is definitely a Nazi, was a Nazi (age is right for Hitler Youth), is the son of Nazis, is a neo-Nazi, or is at least a Nazi sympathizer. I've had to go back to the store several times in the past year. I looked into those stone-cold icy-blue eyes, and they seemed not to be eyes at all but some frozen mineral substance through which every kind of cruelty could be transmitted either in or out. These blue-glass, eyeball-shaped objects could take in information and process it into Nazi ideology instantly. I saw it happening as we spoke. I could see him signing an order, slamming a prison door—worse, but I don't want to say the words, see the words, even think them. I see him at a higher level than prison guard—more of an official, or an assistant in policymaking. I can't see him in the locality of a camp. I see him in an office; he's in between a petty bureaucrat and a high official. I can see him sitting back with his shiny black boots up on the mahogany desk. He's smoking a cigar, drinking a brandy, and smiling while frowning. This is something only a German could do—this complicated facial maneuver. He's turning down requests for passports and exit visas.

What he is doing now in midtown Manhattan (where you and I can't stand to go) among the hordes of inferior racial types I don't dare to imagine. He must be working up his hatred and disgust and collecting names and addresses for the extermination of millions in the future. I remember when you told me that your five-year-old son fell in love with the receptionist there—the one with the dyed-black puffed-out hair and layers of makeup. Imagine why Kropstadt keeps such a specimen in his store.

I had brought in my sunglasses to have the frames copied—as I once did before, with a pair of my husband's frames—since those thin Italian frames aren't made anymore, and Kropstadt said, "I haf to send them to Germany." Imagine my horror. He's German, but his nationality has always been an unspoken fact, and suddenly there he is, out of the skeleton closet, saying the name of that country. There was a period of time in the whole U.S.A. when one wouldn't have dared to have something sent to be made in Germany. Anyone who was German had to hide in Argentina. German products were shunned; there was a dead silence or worse at the mention of anything German. My mother was afraid to

buy one of my older sisters a Steiff teddy bear, though it was
the highest-quality bear made. My mother wanted my sister
to have the best animals to take with her to her college room
at an Ivy League college. "These girls all have Steiff animals
on their beds," my mother explained. We weren't allowed to
have a hairbrush made in Germany, and my father looked ill
when being offered a good buy on a used Mercedes in 1961.

As I imagined my frames being sent to Germany—I could
never consent to this—Kropstadt gave me the price. "It now
costs two hundred and fifty dollars," he said in a cruel, killing
deadpan style, trying with those ice-blue eyeballs to pierce, as
if with sharp daggers, my plan to have my frames copied.
When I asked, "What happened to the man who copied
them in this country for a hundred dollars?" he said, "He
died," still staring at me, his face a cold white stone, his eyes
frozen gray-blue. He said the word "died" in a horrible
way—he may even have had the man murdered. When I said,
"Oh, I was afraid you might say that, because he took so long
to do the work that I assumed he was an old man," Kropstadt
(obviously a false name) said, still with no facial expression,
"Yesss, yesss, he isss too oldt." (Why did he change tense
from past to present?) When I asked him to which city in
Germany he had the frames sent, he said, "Yes, Germany."
When I repeated, "Which city?" he said, "I don't know." He
then added, with a spurt of mental activity or simply the German efficiency his monster race is known for, "The man who
takes the frames iss comink tomorrow morningk, and that iss
your best chance to have it done. He will take them with
him."

I saw the transaction between the two: Kropstadt giving
him the frames, the other German putting them into his

black leather briefcase, a briefcase that might have been used in the nineteen-forties for other kinds of documents. I saw the frames in the briefcase in the airplane over the ocean, then going into the factory—the factory that was used for what in 1944? I said I didn't want to lose the glasses, sending them overseas and all that—couldn't they be copied from a drawing or pattern?—and he said, without any expression on his face or in his voice, "Well, I give the frames to a person, the plane may be hijacked, the person may be shot or killed, the plane's cargo may be destroyed in an explosion, we don't know." He never smiled but looked through my eyes; he must have been trying to see my racial type, German or Austrian, looking for the trace of Semitic blood which would doom me and my family if he were the official in charge. I do have that one grandparent in my genealogy. I imagined asking Kropstadt for the favor of life during the war (though I hadn't been born yet), and saw him thinking that I was good-looking once—just last year—but was now past the bloom of youth, nearing forty. I imagined being called "Fräulein" by his smirking lips. "At one time, Fräulein," he could have said, "I might have been tempted to make a deal, but no longer."

It occurred to me as this was going on that I would have to find a way to get the frames copied at a normal, American optician's, and I would need some glasses to wear while mine were away. It would be all right to buy a quick substitute pair from Osborn's. After all, I had recently been forced by necessity to buy a Braun alarm clock. I put my glasses away and asked Kropstadt about getting new ones to wear in the meantime. "How about those?" I asked, pointing to some thin frames in the next showcase.

"Wait one moment," he said. "I will bring you something. It is in the back room."

What was the urgency about having sunglasses, especially this pair, available in the dead of winter, since I don't even wear prescription glasses—I have perfect vision. In the year during which we haven't seen each other I have aged unbelievably, especially around the eye area, and find that some days the only way I can appear in public or even before any other human being is by wearing these dark glasses. This shape and only this shape out of the thousands now available is perfect for my disintegrating face. As you know, my face has always been slightly misshapen—for this alone I might be condemned by Kropstadt's superiors. On the other hand they often think I'm one of them, and in documentaries shown over and over on A&E, the top henchmen have misshapen faces too.

My facial disintegration began when my mother died, and I started to wear those sunglasses in the days right after that, but they were cold sunny days. Soon I was wearing them on less sunny days, and after a while I was using them as a crutch for everything. Then I almost lost them. When I discovered that they were missing from my bag and my pocket, I got the garage attendants to direct me down to the dungeon where our car was parked. "We don't bring no cars up for people to find things," they said. When I couldn't find them in the car, I went home and fell onto the couch and cried. My husband said, "This is wrong, to be so depressed by lost sunglasses." I told this to the Viennese analyst I was consulting, uselessly, at the time, and he said, "Well, yes, women get more attached to things than men do." I'd never thought of that.

I called Marianne Barnes, the real-estate broker in Roxbury, Connecticut—she was the real-estate broker you recommended. I thought that somehow my precious glasses might have fallen out of my pocket or hand or shoulder bag in the back seat of her real-estate-viewing station wagon as we went bumping over those hilly Connecticut roads, speeding so that one bump made me hit my head really hard on the steel beam of the roof of the wagon.

It was necessary to take the glasses off once we were inside the houses, to see what the insides looked like, and then to put them back on again, to prevent people from seeing what I looked like. I had no hope that the glasses would be in the car, as I had no hope left that we could find a house in Connecticut for under four hundred thousand dollars, but Marianne was so optimistic—saying things like "You should buy the house next to the Presbyterian church; they would love Wasps like you as neighbors"—that I thought I should try. I left a message with her secretary, and Marianne called back the same day. "We found your glasses in a case marked Whittaker's Opticians, Madison Avenue," she said with approval. (You sent me there, too, in 1968, to get thin horn-rimmed frames when they were a rare thing.) She was coming into the city, she said, to buy her three sons Ralph Lauren blazers, shirts, socks—everything—and she would leave my glasses in an envelope at the New York Athletic Club. Her husband was a member of the club.

"They were on the back seat of the wagon," she said. "I went out as soon as I got your message and searched for them. Whittaker's Opticians, Madison Avenue?" she said with a note of hysteria in her voice. That was the right optician for people who are from her section of Connecticut. And just think—it isn't there anymore, it's been taken over by a new generation of young middle-class business thugs; only two of those old genteel gentlemen remain. One of this new bunch told me the lie "That frame isn't made anymore." This is why I had to go to Osborn's. Because Kropstadt would get you anything from anywhere, though his preferred country to trade with was, naturally, Deutschland.

When I heard that Marianne had found my glasses, I was so happy that I had to say in the spirit of joy and relief, "Oh, thank you, you can't imagine what this means to me. And I can tell you how to remove the polo player from your sons' new garments."

"Remove them?" she said. "Why? They want them. Everything must have the polo player—it's a symbol." I knew she could sink low but not that low. I thought she knew she could have bought all the original versions of these clothes at Brooks Brothers, as you did before there was Ralph Lauren, or when Ralph was in high school, before he changed his name. A Hebrew school, I believe he went to, and is only several or fourteen years older than we are. Then Ralph learned the thing he so yearned to be, learned it and copied the whole thing and put it all together—though it can't ever have the authentic look—and then ruined the shirts, with the polo player embroidered right on the chest.

"Why?" I said. "Because the polo player ruins the thing, whatever it is. You can take it off with a seam ripper. It's a sewing instrument, like a small pencil with a tiny blade on the end. You stick the blade under the stitching, starting with a big part, like the horse's body, and working around to the hooves." The horse's legs are thin, and these legs and the mallet are the most difficult parts of the painstaking job—cutting, then tweezing with a slant-edge tweezer the many threads from where they've been cut. Each player takes two to four hours to remove. I removed my first polo player during a hurricane in Nantucket in 1976. Your neck gets stiff from looking down at the thing so long, and on certain thin cotton fabrics there will be a mark where the stitching was. The method can be used with definite success only on cuffs. In all honesty, a shirt with a chest emblem should not be attempted. Don't purchase the shirt, no matter how beautiful the plaid or stripe.

At the New York Athletic Club they couldn't find my glasses. I said that Mrs. Barnes had left them for me in an envelope. I gave my name and spelled it. Maybe they didn't like the name or the spelling of it, maybe they were suspicious, maybe they didn't know it to be Austrian German and knew of a Jewish person with the name. I once saw the obituary of a Catholic priest with the same name. A couple of others with the name were reposing at Frank Campbell's. Services were held for a few at Episcopal churches. But one was alive and was a shopkeeper on Orchard Street. Maybe they didn't like Mrs. Barnes; perhaps she often left packages for her real-estate clients, some of whom were not Christians, and maybe these people were forever picking up and delivering things there, and the employees of the club envisioned this stream of people following Mrs. Barnes to that part of Connecticut. Perhaps she was a main breaker of the gentlemen's agreement—had made it into a thriving business for herself.

I insisted politely that my glasses were there, in an envelope, and I wanted to say, "If you would just get them and give them to me, it would be in your best interests—I'd leave." At last someone went to a back room and found them right away. No apologies were made.

Once the glasses were back in my possession, I thought things over carefully as I inspected them for the future. One sidepiece was cracked, the frame was faded and weak-looking, and I saw that someday they would have to be replaced. This was how I got the idea to have them copied, but since Osborn's was the only place I knew for copying, and it was buried in the part of midtown that's being more crowded out and darkened and squeezed in by new high buildings and workers spilling forth from these buildings, it took me two years to get there. One building over on Madison Avenue appeared to be all cement, without any windows. I had seen it being built for several years, but when I saw the bottom of it completed I didn't know where I was. Was I still on Madison Avenue? Had I somehow gotten onto a side street? Was I in Minneapolis? Was I on the planet Saturn? Where were the buildings of New York that made it look like New York? What had happened to the brain of Philip Johnson?

At Osborn's Opticians, when Kropstadt was in the back room and I tired of looking at my face in the mirror on the display case, my eyes came to rest upon the display case itself. The display was: snow—fake white snow sprinkled on the dark-green fake-velvet fabric in the case, with pairs of eyeglasses perched here and there at peculiar angles in the snow. I thought of the documentaries about the liberation of the concentration camps at the end of the war. How they found piles of clothing—children's, men's, women's, babies', piles of shoes and boots—and cartons of eyeglasses. Sometimes a few of these things were strewn about in odd ways in the grass

or dirt or snow. What did Kropstadt think on the day the display was done? "This iss nice"? Or "How stupid, but we must
go along with the Christmas season, I suppose"? Or "This is
all the doing of the New York merchants, to make Christmas
so commercial. Yess, in Europe it is a religious holiday, I
think"?

He was a bored, tired German on the December day I saw
him. Six feet one or two; light, straight hair, cut short, side-
parted and combed neatly. Cruel slits of blue eyes seeming to
grow larger and bluer as he looked into my eyes—fair skin,
and average teeth, which I saw because he yawned a few
times. He wore a gray suit and a light-blue shirt of some fine-
weave cotton.

When he yawned the second time, he stretched, and I saw
the whole expanse of blue cloth, so fine it had a silken sheen,
and I noticed that he had developed a slight paunch since I
had last been there, a couple of years before. I was surprised,
because when I had first entered the store and looked at him
face-to-face, his face seemed thin, and I had to resist the
urge to say, "You seem thinner." Weight loss didn't seem to
be the right topic to discuss with someone who might have
once been in the starvation business. Or had he gotten it
all into perspective—"Yes, in the war we starved millions,
but now we can speak of weight loss without thinking of this
at all."

The man was extremely bored by trying to find a replacement frame for me, though I made it easy for him. I didn't
want to spend the day in his shop. I wanted to get out while
the sun was setting so I could walk up to the park, and into
the twilight. Although I knew millions had been deprived of

seeing another sunset or twilight ever again, I didn't think to sacrifice the experience by sitting and staring into this man's eyes and taking in what his countrymen had done.

He lazily brought forth a round tray of frames I'd never seen at any other optician's. It was a tray of fifty frames, all one style, each a different color, the purpose being to allow the customers to see all the colors available in this particular frame. Only the Germans could think up such a grotesque concept. I picked up a blue-green sample and held it in front of my eyes. "I can just get this in the meantime," I said. He was looking at the color and shape—in disagreement, I could tell from his deadly stare. "She could be my prisoner, and here I am providing frame-color advice to her," he must have been thinking.

"And what about the lens color?" he asked.

"How about the same as my old ones?" I asked.

"These are the colors we have," he said, bringing forward a tray of about thirty colored discs, none of which was the color of my lenses.

"Mine are blue-green-gray," I said. Unhappily he took a gray disc and flipped it onto a small white round paper he apparently used just for this purpose. The Germans are always inventing things. With a flick of his wrist, he placed a blue disc on top. I took a green one and put it on that. When the color looked close, I said, O.K., that's fine, could you please have them done? I didn't like being involved in such close collaboration with him, in spite of his technical skills.

I got up to make my escape, when I happened to see in the last showcase of snowflakes a pair of high-quality clip-on sunglass lenses. I couldn't believe my good fortune. In

Nantucket, where I usually buy a cheap brand called Clip-pettes at the drugstore, they no longer carried them, and on very sunny days I had to wear a scratched-up, dulled pair on top of my Italian sunglasses, though I could barely see through them anymore. I asked Kropstadt to show me the clip-ons, and he said he thought there must be another pair in the back room. Again the back room. "Would they fit on these glasses?" I asked, taking them out again. He put the lenses on—they were the wrong size and shape—and handed them to me, obviously thinking what a bad idea they were. "Oh, good," I said. "Can I buy these?"

"Wait, just one moment and I will see if there is another." When he returned from the back, he was miserably polishing up a pair. He put them in their cheap plastic case, and I paid for them. "We will call you when we have your others ready," he said. "Maybe in one week."

Finally out onto Park Avenue; the afternoon light was gone; there was no twilight, just grayness, and the throngs of office workers from those new buildings spilling out into the streets and dingy sidewalks. How could I have spent the most beautiful hour of the day discussing frames with Kropstadt? What a waste my life was.

I stood on the corner wondering which street was worse to walk up, Park or Madison. Hundreds of humans came toward me as I finally chose and walked to Madison. I soon came face-to-face with the all-cement building. I thought to hurry across to Fifth Avenue but knew it could be even more crowded there. Instead I walked up to Fifty-seventh as fast as I could and then over to Fifth, where I found the sky waiting, empty, across from the Plaza Hotel and everywhere above the park. I walked up Fifth on the park side, looking into the sky and thinking about the fact that I was transacting business with a German.

One day right before Christmas, a man with a European accent called on the phone and asked for me. I admitted to being myself instead of saying that I was my secretary and that I was out. "Your eyeglasses are ready," the accent said. It was not Kropstadt but one of his aides. "Can you please pick them up within the week?"

"I'm sorry, but I'm going to be away until after New Year's," I said.

"Could you try to pick them up during the next few days?" the voice said. The thought of going to midtown Manhattan the week before Christmas and especially the week after is a terrifying thought, with the added millions in from other states and planets to see the tree. Only David Letterman has the sense to announce every year that there is no tree, stay home, look at your own tree in your own town, but nobody pays heed to his command. Why couldn't he be Mayor? Or at least President?

It was true that I was going to be away that week. I'd arranged to be out of the city as many weeks as possible, especially when it was over forty degrees or more crowded than usual. The accent was disappointed.

The next call was from Kropstadt. I have to say I enjoyed hearing his voice on the answering machine in January. It was becoming a dangerous game. I left the message on the machine for my husband to hear, but he got no excitement from it, though he knew the whole story.

January went by, February, too, and as we got into March I knew I had almost no time left if I was ever going to get to midtown Manhattan before the heat and humidity started, as they now do in April, due to the greenhouse effect and the hole in the ozone layer, which are both happening this minute and not, as was first predicted, in a hundred years. The world meltdown has begun. Still, I let part of March go by, until I had to go to a dentist appointment in Rockefeller Center—another feared midtown location. I went this once to a very mean dentist, who seemed to be a man on the verge of suicide. You've read that dentists have the highest suicide rate? Not high enough, I say. But this one appeared to be simply following a psychiatrist's orders: "Go to work, keep up a routine, X-ray teeth, poke at fillings, drill teeth, fill them, continue your normal life, stay on the antidepressant medication, and come in for psychiatric visits every day." The man didn't even have the patience to listen to which tooth was the problem. As I tried to say second from the back on the lower left, the man had to stare away in a state of subdued rage. I saw it in his eyes, and when he drilled away at an old filling he threw his dental instruments onto my chest instead of the little dental worktable—he threw them hard; he probably wanted to stab me with them. He even threw the drill.

When I went back to the periodontist who'd recommended this dentist, I told him about the experience, and he said, "Well, he's moody. He's Hungarian." I explained about the throwing of the instruments, and he said sometimes a dentist would place an instrument on a patient's chest, but when I said "The drill?" he could only shake his head and repeat "The drill?"

Is that called moody, when the mood is one of contemplating suicide? Not that I knew this for a fact, but what else could it have been? I caught a glimpse of his trouser cuffs—

bell-bottoms—and his shoes—gold-adorned black loafers. These alone are bad signs, especially for a sixty-five-year-old dentist. I once rejected another sixty-five-year-old endodontist for wearing a gold chain, bell-bottoms, and white patent-leather loafers. Later on I found out that he was an eminent endodontist whom my conservative, more eminent periodontist allowed to do a root canal on his own tooth.

I had searched for the right endodontist for a year, while a nerve was slowly dying in a three-canal molar, because think about it: What is root-canal therapy?

This is why you must have total distraction to transcend the endodontic experience—you need a view of Central Park from the dental chair, you must be in a perfectly clean, white, sterile room with a clean beige or light-gray waiting room, a no-smoking sign, a few flowers on the desk, and a Mozart opera to listen to on your stereo earphones. These things aid transcending. The endodontist should be a dentist from the past, neat and clean without extra or long hair. He can't wear jewelry.

I finally found such a man, the right endodontist; in fact he criticized *my* footwear—running sneakers—and I explained that I needed them to walk miles into Central Park after the appointment, but he shook his head with no understanding. Before the nerve died, the endodontist died. His partner took over—an even more conservative nineteen-fifties kind of dentist, a Catholic Republican from Westchester who had nothing to say about anything. There was no sympathy to be gotten from this man, just "All right" when he had finished the grueling session. Sometimes I was sorry when it ended, because I was in the middle of *Così Fan Tutte,* but other times, when I said I could feel some pain, he said,

"You don't feel pain, you feel the pressure." Once, when I asked, "What is that flaming hot poker that goes into the tooth at the end?" he almost smiled as he said, "To burn away the evil spirits."

Leaving the moody Hungarian's office, I noticed this Republican endodontist's name on another door—it was the eighteenth floor, a floor of all dentists. He'd had to move and give up his Central Park view. The dark-gray hallways were silent, but each dark door had a few names with D.D.S. after them. Imagine a whole floor and long hallways of all dentists. Imagine the accumulated fear, anxiety, and pain felt on that floor hour after hour, day after day, year after year.

It was in that spirit that I left the building in March, and found myself on Fifth Avenue, only a few blocks from Osborn's Opticians. I should go over and get my replacement glasses, I thought as I started the walk to Park Avenue. I'd been wearing the old sunglasses all this time to keep the dental headlights from blinding me. I peered in first, to see if Kropstadt was about, but he was not. I entered the shop and spotted the only civilized-looking human being who worked there—the small fearful Belgian, Mr. Frey. Until you told me he was Belgian I could only wonder about the accent; it was the first European accent to leave a message on the machine. How do we know he's Belgian? Is the fearfulness based on guilt? Is he simply timid? Is he afraid of Kropstadt, or does he have something to hide? Still, I took to him immediately, because he was getting bald but had the good sense to brush what hair he had all straight back—Here it is, the forehead, the receding line, the scalp, so what?—rather than parting it lower down on the side of the head and trickily brushing it over to conceal the recession, the way Gary Hart did. This was never mentioned—that *this* was why you couldn't trust Gary Hart, a presidential candidate who thinks people are fooled by covering the baldness with hair from another part of the head. He dared to mention John F. Kennedy as his hero and mentor, but just compare the two heads of hair. Only I spoke about it, only *I* said I never trusted him, because of the hair cover-up, and a suspected nose job, plus a pinky ring. All those who trusted him got what they deserved in disappointment. They also never speak of Yassir Arafat's many nose jobs when he is mentioned. Or maybe it was only one job, where the thick sides were hacked away and two deep indentations remain. People are aghast when I bring this up. Once I said, "Am I the only one to have noticed this?" They all laughed. There was incredulousness in the laughter. They couldn't think of Yassir Arafat this way. But just look at him on TV— it's the first thing you notice, other than his filthy turban and perpetual three-day growth of beard.

Mr. Frey said he was afraid he wouldn't be able to find my glasses because so much time had gone by, but he found them right away. "Let me see," he said, looking for my name in the small index file on the desk. The suspense is always: Will they pronounce it American or will they pronounce it German? Now he was doing the American style, with only the faintest of accents. As soon as he found them, I saw that the glasses were a mistake. They looked bright blue, deep blue, and so did the lenses. I tried them on; they looked even worse. I said I'd better change the color of the lenses, but I didn't have time to look at them all, could I come back? He said all right, but they looked good to him the way they were. On the way

out, I thought I saw Kropstadt hovering around near the door
to the back room.

The next week—it was still March—the periodontist told me
he was moving his offices to Park Avenue, two blocks from
Osborn's. He had to leave Fifth Avenue and Fifty-seventh
Street after forty years because his building was now owned
by Imelda Marcos and he couldn't get more space there for
his many new periodontal partners. This meant I wouldn't
get to see the view of the sky and the treetops in Central Park
in April. And I would be forced deep into midtown every
three months for sure, and probably even every other month,
for emergencies involving one tooth where the gum and
bone were botched by an oral surgeon twenty years ago in his
attempt to chop out a wisdom tooth impacted in the jawbone, although it should have been left there, since it wasn't
causing any trouble. In fact, all my periodontic and endodontic travels are connected to that one mistake. One man's need
to earn a hundred and fifty dollars wherever he could, and a
lifetime of dental excursions for the patient.

Even before another of these emergencies could develop, at
the end of March, my husband looked at his eyeglass frames
and noticed they were cracking and weakening in several
places. "Do I have a spare pair?" he asked me. What a joke. As
if he'd have a spare of anything, with his suit pants worn to
shreds in the seat, his collars frayed, his ties unraveling. He has
no time to attend to these things, though his office is right
smack in the midtown neighborhood. "What do I do, just take
these into Osborn's and get another pair?" he asked. Just take
them into Osborn's! Had he no recollection of the compli-

cated procedure we'd been through with Kropstadt a few years before to get this pair? They were the kind of frames Communists and intellectuals wore in the nineteen-thirties, the kind that were beginning to be in demand by kids our age in the nineteen-sixties and seventies. These were round and were called flesh-tinted, but I never saw skin that color. They were given out by the British government health service for several decades, the way wire-rimmed round ones were given out by the United States government. English friends of ours would stare politely and say, "Where'd you get those? They're British Health Service frames here, you know." We had found a crooked optician on Madison Avenue who had bunches of old frames from the thirties and forties, and he was selling them at high prices, considering that they were several decades old, even in 1978. You couldn't get your exact size but had to take whatever fit best. The frames would fall apart in a few months. If you took them back, he'd say you had to buy another pair.

Soon optical companies caught on to the demand and began reproducing the frames, but they were never quite right. Osborn's had the right shape, but the wrong color— clear plastic. "We will haf to dye it for you," Kropstadt said. First he had to search the frame archives. "I haf found it," he declared, "but it is made only in clear." He took out his tray of magic lenses and put one on his magic white paper, showing that they could dye the frames the same way. "Fifty percent tan," he said, taking one. "Or eighty percent tan," he said, showing us another, slightly more tan lens. "I think fifty percent is closest to the original."

We agreed to fifty percent. He was right—it all worked out as he planned.

But then a couple of years went by, maybe three, and it was time for new ones. They'd been dropped a lot. Picture this: A man takes his glasses off and reaches over to place them on his night table but misses and they land on the pine floor. This happens every week for a year. Sometimes the man takes off the glasses in order to wash his face. He puts them on the towel rack by sticking the earpiece behind the towel rack on the tile wall. He turns to reach for a towel and knocks them onto the tile floor. The frames last through all this, the lenses, too. But then eventually everything weakens and a visit to Osborn's is necessary. We're told, "The frame is no longer made. We can get one from a different company, but it won't be quite as thin." Seeing my alarm, Kropstadt says, "We can have them filed down. In our workroom in the back. We have special machinery." They have special machinery. "The cost depends on how thin you want them and how long it takes to do the filing."

We agreed to the maximum filing, and once again the results were as predicted by the expert. But time continues and this is something I still don't understand. How does time continue? When you were a child it was the same time—time moved as it moves now—but then you were young and now you're forty. How does this happen? I can't find out, because no bookstore has a copy of *Matter and Memory*. I can call the publisher, which is nearby, on the corner of Broadway and Houston. I must have passed it many times on my walks in SoHo, wasting my life searching for organically grown carrots. If I get hold of a copy, will I ever understand the passage of time? Is it only that when you were a child time was on your side? Where was time before you were born? On your side then, certainly, too. But now no longer. Now on the other side. And this is how it got to be time for new frames. And how Kropstadt's hair was not blond, as it once was, but almost white. Silvery white.

I made a practice visit late one afternoon, when I saw that Brooks Brothers and Paul Stuart had closed. Osborn's would be closed too. I went up to the window and stared in. I went around to the front door. The window gates were down, but the lights were on. There he was. He was busy. Busy, busy at work. Moving this and that and something from here to there. He noticed me looking in as he worked, but he avoided looking back. I saw something I'd never seen before—his jaw was clenched, and there was a slight muscle spasm in his cheek. Not that slight. As I watched him work, it happened a few times. It must have been this: He recognized me or remembered someone who looked like me in Germany. In Vienna, more likely—he'd known or seen one of my ancestors. He was afraid I had something on him, I know it because of the jaw-clenching. But all I wanted was more frames. I scurried off in a Kafka-like mode. Since I was wearing running sneakers, the scurrying was simplified.

I went back one day at 5 P.M. in early April. It was getting serious with my husband's glasses. He was asking about them nightly. "What do I do about glasses?" he'd say, looking at his crumpled frames.

Kropstadt was sitting at his station in the back—the general's seat. He was with a customer. I went straight up to the timid Belgian and handed him the old frames. Lucky for me, he seemed to have forgotten all about my frames, the bright-blue mistake that had been intended to substitute for my Italian frames that Kropstadt had wanted to send to Germany

months before. "I have to find his chart," Frey said. His chart.
What is written on this chart? He was spelling my husband's
Austrian last name but not inquiring about the country of
origin. At least not aloud. I took this opportunity to give
Kropstadt a sideward glance from my table across the store.
He was engrossed in lively conversation with the customer,
an average sixty-year-old rich lady from the Upper East Side.
"For years my wife wore these," he said about some glasses.

Then the customer said something about wearing them
playing golf, but I was thinking about Kropstadt's having a
wife. I had never thought of this before. He might be part of
a family.

They were talking about some particular frames. He
became more animated and enthusiastic—not the way he is
when talking to me. There's no rapport and exchange of
familial preference of frame styles between us. "It is steel," I
heard him say next. "The whole frame is molded to my head.
It costs twelve hundred dollars." I couldn't believe my ears. I
grabbed a business card from the desk and wrote down what
he said.

Then I saw myself in the round desk mirror. I had the
worst cold I'd ever had. I'd told the periodontist to wear a
mask while he scraped at the back molar root. I couldn't miss
an appointment there, no matter what. They sent a card the
week before, to remind you of the appointment. They called
you the day before. They warned you not to be late. Everything was a hundred dollars—everything minor, that is. The
chronic problem with the tooth root, though, was what kept
leading me back to the neighborhood of Osborn's.

I couldn't believe how tired I looked. It was a wonder that
anyone would have anything to do with me. How kind peo-

ple could be. I seemed to have aged several years in the last two weeks. Was this what it was to have a cold? I couldn't remember, rarely having had one, due to macrobiotic living. I wanted to get out of there and not subject anyone to my presence any further. Frey came back with the information and said he'd call in the order.

He smiled a polite European smile, and I smiled weakly back. He said he'd call me when the frames came in. If any filing or dyeing was necessary we would decide at that time. Then, suddenly, just for a moment, it all seemed to be nothing. The Belgian had me fooled with his soothing accent and honest hair style. You see, I thought for an instant, all it was was this—Kropstadt just loved his work. He loved frames and glasses and lenses and getting the right solution to a difficult problem. He was in the eyeglass business. He was a simple, upper-middle-class businessman. He was good at his job. He had a special interest in it. That's it. He was just a lens-and-frame nut. Maybe I'd misunderstood the whole thing. No. It was the cold virus weakening my powers of observation.

In any case, I know you favor this optician and I thought you would want to be warned and go elsewhere, no matter how many frames they have and what fine work they do. At what cost, you may ask yourself.

Christmas Wishes to you and your family. And Happy New Year, too.

Do the Windows Open?

For several years I was afraid to ride the South Fork Bus. Then one day I rode it. The day itself was over, since I couldn't get my courage up for the afternoon bus to New York, but I did make it to the 7 P.M. For one year I had driven myself back and forth from East Hampton to New York. It had taken me ten years to try this. Then, all of a sudden, after almost mastering it, I could never do it again.

Even when I drove the better but longer way onto the Northern State Parkway and across the Triborough Bridge and down the F.D.R. Drive to get to my apartment in SoHo, the trip was still horrible and I couldn't keep doing it. Once I crossed that bridge at night in a thunderstorm with cars speeding past me on the left and right. But it was the part of the Grand Central Parkway near La Guardia that started to cause the attacks of no breathing. Nothing like the more serious attacks of paralysis of the lungs that occurred when I took the worse route—the Long Island Expressway and the deadly approach to the Midtown Tunnel, with trucks passing on the right and three lanes of headlights coming toward me on the left.

On one of my last trips a single truck caused a severe attack. How could I have thought I could drive among trucks? How many trucks could there be at night? was my reasoning. There could be a whole highway full of trucks at night on the Long Island Expressway, and one of these trucks in front of me had an open cargo, if it could be called a cargo—a load of dust. Dust was its cargo, probably asbestos dust was what it was filled with, and this asbestos dust wasn't packed up in barrels and tied down but simply heaped onto the back and covered with a thin gray sheet. The sheet wasn't even tied down, so it flapped around and the dust was blowing into the air, and there was no way to see through these gusts of asbestos dust.

I'll pass the truck, I thought—because I had learned how to pass with *Così Fan Tutte* playing on the radio for encouragement, but I quickly discovered that I hadn't learned to pass on a curve with no visibility, no matter what opera of Mozart's was on and no matter how loud. I was trying to pass the asbestos truck on the left, I had the signal on, only a few seconds had gone by while I was waiting for a part of the road that wasn't curved. But whenever one came up, the dust would start to blow, and it would be a case of trying to pass into dust through dust to nowhere. As I waited these few seconds with Karl Böhm conducting, cars began to squeeze in and pass on the right. Couldn't they tell that I was going to pass at the correct moment?

My last trip took place on a rainy night. Although I had listened to the weather reports all day and they had warned of only occasional light rain, heavy rain overtook the road at the safe, wide, empty part east of Manorville. Before I could get into the right lane, a gigantic blue-and-white vehicle roared past, going sixty or seventy, splashing water so that I was completely blinded for several seconds. This vehicle was the South Fork Bus. I thought, It would be better to be on the South Fork Bus than to be passed on the right by it in a rainstorm.

I prepared myself for that first trip on the bus by seeing someone else off. The passenger I chose to see off was my husband. "It's not so bad," I said when I got to see the bus. Nothing is so bad if it isn't summer. The people, the things they have with them, namely, their faces, their bodies, their hairstyles—none of this is so bad in cold weather. But even as I said that it wasn't so bad I noticed that the seats were too close together, and I couldn't help wondering what it would be like to be aboard when the vehicle filled up with human beings and departed from pleasant, tree-lined Main Street. When it got *onto the road. Onto the road,* with fifty other humans and their paraphernalia. *Onto the Expressway.* The thought filled me with horror.

My husband didn't mind his time on the bus. He said, "I work, I read, I sleep. It's great—I'm not driving."

I would never be able to work, read, or sleep. I was working on a series of photographs of flowers in decline, and there wouldn't be any plants or flowers on the bus. My other project was to photograph the reproductive surgeon Dr. Arnold Loquesto with his dog, and they wouldn't be on the bus, either. Reading in vehicles caused nausea, and sleeping on a bus on a highway was insane. "Are there seat belts?" I asked my husband.

"No. Why? You mean you're afraid to ride the South Fork Bus?"

"Not afraid. Do the windows open?"

"No. Windows on these new things don't open anymore. Why—you need the windows to open?"

"It would be better if they could be opened."

"Who wants to open the windows on the Long Island Expressway?" he said.

As the departure time approached for my first trip on the bus, I thought that this must be the way people feel when waiting to board a plane. They're always telling us that cars are more dangerous than planes. Why not be afraid of both? I'll take half a Xanax to enable me to get aboard, I decided. A dentist had prescribed some for a root-extraction session, and I had eleven pills left. People I knew were always trying to get the Xanax away from me for themselves. One of these people was an anxiety-filled flower arranger. During a discussion of highway driving, he mentioned that he couldn't drive on the Expressway at all. He told me this with a look of fear in his large, blue, flower-arranging eyes. These driving conversations had made him my favorite person to talk to from Southampton to East Hampton. "The traffic will be over by six, but then it will be dark," he said. "Aren't you afraid to drive in the dark?"

"It's not the dark. It's the headlights," I said.

"Yes! The headlights! Forget it. I can't even do it in the daylight. My last time I broke into a sweat, the panic started, and when I got to the city I ran to St. Patrick's to say a prayer."

I had confided in a religious, panic-stricken flower arranger. Which was more scary, his religious fervor or his descriptions of floral arrangements for funerals? Both gave me shivers.

I felt brave as I waited out in the cold night for the South Fork Bus. Very few people waited with me. This bus is so big, I thought—it must be safer than a car. "We're the biggest thing on the road," a confident middle-aged male passenger said to everyone in a spirit of camaraderie as the bus came down the street. But I was not the comrade of any of the passengers on the South Fork Bus, I thought as I watched them board on that first dark winter night.

I determined that the safest seat would be on the right and in the middle. In a crash the front of the bus would fold up, crunching together the driver and the first few rows. The left side would go into those three lanes of oncoming headlights I had studied during my own driving experiences. The back would smash together if the bus was hit from behind. The middle could jackknife, but I'd heard that this kind of accident was rare.

The back seats were near the bathroom, and an important rule in traveling and in dining out is to avoid sitting near plumbing. Yet, even with this rule seeming to make perfect sense, certain passengers on the South Fork Bus chose the bathroom corner as their most desired place to sit. After watching a series of almost normal-looking individuals head for various sections of the middle and front, I saw that a tall man, all in black leather, was heading right for the seat across from the dreaded bathroom door. He was between fifty and sixty, and almost bald—he had some hair, but it was very short and gray. Probably he was a member of some sado-masochist-black-leather Hampton set, the first of his kind I'd ever seen. The minute he got to the back I heard a loud cough. Not a normal cough. A loud, choking, screaming kind of cough. Maybe his choosing the back seat was simply a matter of wanting to cough alone, to save his fellow passengers the experience of hearing this cough at closer range, and to preserve whatever dignity a black-leather sado man could have. Before everyone was seated he coughed again. Other people were getting scared, not just me. I figured I had gotten to the normal amount of fear with that half a Xanax in my brain. I saw that some hadn't even noticed the cough and were getting themselves ready for the trip with their newspapers and shopping bags and parcels.

People were making themselves comfortable—they didn't think that this was going to be their last day on earth. One woman had a special neck pillow, another had a lap robe. Others had beverages—coffee, tea, and juice. Although the South Fork Bus was known for giving out Perrier, these passengers couldn't wait. They had magazines and books, and about half of them had headphones. The other half were going to take naps. Naps were planned for the Long Island Expressway! I saw people adjusting their seats backward into other people's knee space. Certain passengers were polite and consulted the people behind them, others did whatever they pleased. Supposedly in warmer weather, when I was in Massachusetts or Maine, fights broke out about this and other things.

The first step I had to take to get ready was to tie myself into my seat with the belt from my reversible alpaca coat. I will have to remember to take this alpaca seat belt off the armrests when I arrive in Manhattan, I thought, because it would be impossible to get another. The one thing of value that I had learned from seeing a Viennese psychiatrist in his newly restored Art Deco building on Central Park West was information on how to obtain this coat. As I went up in the splendid elevator I couldn't help staring at the coat on a woman who looked around my age—at the time, thirty-nine. She was kind enough to tell me the name of a store in England, and several overseas phone calls enabled me to have the same kind of coat. Having read that the wrong style seat belt can be more dangerous than none at all, I knew that this was the wrong style, the kind that causes ruptured spleens and herniated other organs. Still I kept to my plan and tied one end of the belt to the outer armrest and the other end to the center armrest.

Next I'd get some Mozart into my earphones—I would add Mozart to my brain, along with the Xanax. This winning combination had helped me through dental surgery, where they have a new device—a pellet gun to shoot bullets of Novocain into the roof of the mouth. It had helped me not to faint as I heard and felt those bullets shoot in.

I had decided that this trip wouldn't require a Mozart opera. A piano sonata would be enough—a trio, a string quartet, or a divertimento might work. Before I could get my earphones on, the South Fork Bus hostess appeared. She announced her name, and began giving the rules of the South Fork Bus. She must have graduated from the est program or some kind of mind-training course, because she was so overly agreeable and pleasant that there had to be a reason for it. "She's an est graduate," I remembered my haircutter, Francine, saying of a certain hair-streaker when I asked, "Why is she so cheerful?"

"You mean it's that fake cheer?" I said.

"More or less," she said. "At first we couldn't stand it, but then we got used to it." Unlike Francine, I couldn't get used to things.

How had the hostess come to the point in life where she could stand to ride back and forth on the Long Island Expressway, I wondered. Maybe, before her trips, she smoked several ounces of marijuana to keep herself from wondering the same thing. Because even the est in her background wouldn't have been enough to allow her to act this way.

Then there was the driver—a middle-aged, red-haired woman who looked as if she had just spent the day in front of a TV, smoking packs of Camels and drinking soda in preparation for her long drive on the South Fork Bus, where smoking was not allowed, "and that includes the rest room." I was thankful for the rule, and I thought I had so many things to be grateful for that if I survived the trip I might run to St. Patrick's, too.

Just into the andante grazioso—I was tied in tightly—I saw that the hostess had made her way up the aisle and was being argued with by a spoiled-looking sixty-year-old man in a heavy, gray, hand-knitted sweater. The passenger wanted to be allowed to use his eastbound ticket to ride westbound. This was strictly forbidden, but the passenger had a reason why it shouldn't be forbidden in his case. The hostess had twisted herself into a position of sympathy and understanding, bending over the passenger with her head tilted and her body turned so that the passenger in back of her was only an inch or two from her hip. "It's really something that we're not allowed to do in any case, but I understand why you think your case is different, and you know what, I *am* going to do it, but if this were ever known I would lose my job—not that this should be anything for you to concern yourself with." Perhaps the marijuana had kicked in to the point where she'd lost all concept of time and didn't realize how long this conversation was going on.

As I watched the other passengers calmly paying their fares, it occurred to me that most of the men on the left side of the bus looked like antiques dealers. The proportion seemed greater than the proportion viewed in other activities around the town. The junk-bond traders from Southampton hadn't yet boarded. When they did get on, they'd be angry that the good seats had been taken by this kind of passenger. But at least then it would be time to get that Perrier. The hostess had promised this.

Passengers at Southampton turned out to have more materialistic and less intellectual paraphernalia than passengers from East Hampton. One woman with short platinum-blond hair had five big shopping bags from the Saks Fifth Avenue Southampton branch, and she was in an angry mood. She'd been drinking. I could smell the alcohol particles in the air.

She was one of those fifty-five-year-old women who always wear black or red, or both together. A red cashmere turtleneck sweater—everything else, including the coat she carried, was black—and all those pieces of jewelry I couldn't identify except for the Rolex and Cartier watches. She had one of each, plus several other kinds of gold bracelets. She was sitting right across the aisle, so I could study her jewelry during the rest of the trip if I needed to.

At last, it was time for the refreshments. But not only wasn't it Perrier, it was some cheap club soda in a plastic bottle and served in plastic cups. All along I had thought that it was going to be an individual green glass bottle for everyone. The hostess was asking people if they wanted little bags of peanuts. She even asked some, "Would you like two?" Several were saying yes. One antiques dealer—he looked like an expert on Biedermeier armoires—had to ask if he could have two. Just the kind of thing I was afraid of but hadn't imagined—soon the entire bus smelled from peanuts. How long would the peanut situation last with the poor ventilation system was something I couldn't get off my mind. Why hadn't these people heard that peanuts are contaminated by the carcinogenic mold aflatoxin?

I noticed that other men had just as poor peanut-eating styles as my husband. Maybe my husband was not so bad. Maybe men are like this, as my exercise teacher, a modern dancer, used to tell me. One man emptied the bag of peanuts into his hand, then threw them all at once into his mouth. Another one held the opened packet to his mouth with his head back and tapped the packet to get the peanuts out.

The time had come to complain about the temperature. It was about one hundred degrees in the bus. People were tearing off their cashmere scarves and sweaters. "We're trying to control the heat," the hostess said. "I know it's awful." Soon there was no heat. The platinum-blond, jewelry-laden passenger was getting angrier as she put her black coat on. I saw that she was eating peanuts, even though she needed to lose ten pounds—her wrists were fattened up under her gold watches. One of the antiques dealers didn't mind the wildly fluctuating temperature conditions, but he was complaining that his overhead light didn't aim right on his newspaper.

Somewhere around Manorville, the hostess made an announcement. "As you may have noticed, we're having a lot of trouble temperaturewise," she said. "We can't control the heat, but we want you all to know that we're trying." Unfortunately, I had taken my earphones off to hear this announcement. Now I had the word "temperaturewise" stamped into my brain, and I also realized that the coughing man was still coughing at timed intervals. It wasn't a real cough, I suddenly knew, but a sign of Tourette's syndrome, where the afflicted person involuntarily shouts obscenities without any control. This man had mastered the cough as a disguise, or he hadn't yet reached the obscenity stage. Perhaps it began with a cough—I couldn't recall, although this was my husband's favorite disease to read about.

Still, this was a better way to ride than driving myself, I thought, even though it was one hundred degrees for half the trip and thirty for the other half. I decided I would become a regular rider of the South Fork Bus throughout the winter. No one noticed when I untied myself from my seat.

Then there was the trip back. Nobody had told me what it was like to board the South Fork Bus at Fortieth Street and Third Avenue. I had only my husband's version of the facts, which was "It's right near my office—a perfect short walk." But, then, the opinion of an architect who would choose to spend his life in the ugliest part of midtown—what is the opinion of this man worth? There are so many hideous office buildings in midtown now, and his is the worst. When you see this building you can think only one thing. "WHY?" is the thing. "Why? Why? Why?" But when you read architects' explanations of why this or that is in their plans, they have answers.

Why can't buildings be built according to the specifications of Prince Charles, I thought when first I saw the sight of East Fortieth Street. Why can't Prince Charles be in charge? East Fortieth Street was filled with gigantic new gray-and-black buildings—if the sky was blue on any day, there would be no way to see it.

A commandant from the bus company was lining up the prisoners in some kind of cavernous space on East Fortieth Street—it wasn't clear what the space was, but some architect must have described it as something. It was like a mall space without any stores, thus combining the worst parts of city life and suburb life. The commandant was drinking coffee out of a plastic-foam cup. He had a look that identified his origins as Montauk and Poland. Yet he was in charge here, with a little smile that could have meant the buses weren't headed for any part of Long Island.

As I looked around I saw that I was trapped, waiting on East Fortieth Street in a cavernous nowhere surrounded by midtown. I was gripped by a fear of the thought of what it would be like to stroll aimlessly through this part of Manhattan. When in midtown, always have a purpose and walk rapidly between appointments, to work, and on errands. In this way you can't be overwhelmed, overtaken, by the mammoth emptiness of square gray spaces and buildings. Your tiny remnant of a soul is crushed into a fragment of itself by traveling the streets of New York—but it can't be obliterated if you keep walking. Walk briskly, ride, leave town if it's over forty degrees, wear dark glasses if the sun is out, stay near Central Park on the Upper East Side, never go to a business district on weekends, never even be in New York on a weekend. Friday isn't safe, either—don't let yourself imagine what it would feel like to be on Park Avenue and Forty-sixth Street on a Sunday in the summer. You would be the only one there—maybe a lost tourist or a derelict in a state of delirium tremens would be someone to share the bleak corner with. Your view would include a building designed to incorporate metal scaffolding into its façade.

By talking to the commandant as if I had normal, casual thoughts on my mind, I found out that the bus was on the way down from the Seventy-third Street stop: the better, Upper East Side, first stop. I knew that the passengers who had boarded there would have that smug first-stop look on their privileged Upper East Side faces. But when the bus pulled up I saw that some of them had chosen the dangerous first-row seats. How stupid people could be, even if they lived on the Upper East Side. It was then I decided that in the future I'd go uptown to Seventy-third Street, in order to board the bus with this smug group.

On the trips from Long Island to New York, I discovered that any kind of person could get on the bus at any stop. One ride from East Hampton started out well. It was still cold out, and almost like a real winter day from the past. It was nearly dusk and I could see out the window that the sky looked as if it might snow, but I knew that in the new greenhouse weather this wasn't likely. As I waited for the bus to start, I was thinking about the movie *The Stranger,* the part where the pharmacist says to Orson Welles, the Nazi Franz Kindler: "Looks like it's coming up for snow." My view of the sky and my happy memory of that film were both suddenly obstructed by a six-foot-six creature who looked exactly like Frankenstein's monster, except for the expression on his face, which was kind and sweet. He did have that protruding frontal bone in his forehead, but his forehead was small and low. He had to fold up his long arms and legs in order to get into the tiny space provided by the bus company for the passengers, the way you have to fold a marionette to get it into its little box. I felt sorry for the man as I noticed his long wristbones sticking out of his jacket sleeves, which were several inches too short. His trousers were a few inches too short, also. He sat down in the seat across from mine. He wore a reddish-brown box-plaid suit and a lopsided Frankenstein-style toupee, the same color brown as his suit. The toupee was tilted too far forward, and, underneath it, in back, his own hair was visible—darker brown with gray. I'd seen this kind of toupee mistake on other men, including something I thought I saw on Dennis Hopper. The box-plaid colors of his suit were turquoise blue and orange. He wore an orange shirt and white socks with turquoise blue stripes around the tops to match it all together. Before long he took out a bag with his lunch or dinner. The meal appeared to be a liverwurst sandwich, and after eating the sandwich he ate two bananas. Then he took out a bag of Pepperidge Farm cookies. When I checked to see which kind of Pepperidge Farm cookie such a man would choose, I was surprised to see that it was Chessmen. In my lifelong acquaintance with this brand of cookie I had never seen anyone buy or eat Chessmen. The Frankenstein man ate about half a bag of Chessmen and then began to read the *Times Book Review.* He was a big man, he had to eat a lot, I tried to tell myself. Still, there could never be a good reason to eat liverwurst, or animals in any form.

After a while I found out that bad things could happen at East Seventy-third Street, too. A woman with a German accent was complaining, in a voice between crying and screaming, about the "air conditions," and the journey had not yet even begun. The woman was about forty-eight but still had long, straight black hair and bangs, as if it were the nineteen-sixties and she were twenty. "What is that terrible odor?" she was asking the driver in her hysterical voice. Other passengers joined in.

"It's food," one said. "People are eating lunch."

"It's something else, in addition to that—it's some kind of fumes!" she said.

People quickly skipped over what it was to how they could avoid this trip on the South Fork Bus. Two elderly gentlemen in suede jackets with fringes said that you could get on the train and still avoid Penn Station by taking a taxi over the Fifty-ninth Street Bridge to Hunter's Point, the place the Long Island Railroad started from—probably some barren, deadly yard in Queens where gangland shoot-outs and drug transactions took place.

Down in the dirty, gray Forties, the first-stop people were becoming aware of the air problem, but before a rebellion could start, the bus stopped and the doors opened to let in the angry midtown line. Before things could settle down I heard sounds of a scuffle a few rows behind me. It sounded like punching noises—maybe two men had started to hit each other. I didn't want to see. The reason for the fight turned out to be that one passenger refused to allow a new passenger to sit next to him. The new passenger, a dark-skinned man, took this to be a racial insult. The seated man explained that he needed two seats for himself because he was tall.

After the altercation was over I heard some swearing and heavy breathing, but I couldn't tell which was coming from which passenger. A light-skinned, sixty-year-old African-Spanish-American woman tried to keep the insulted man calm by turning back toward his seat and reciting outdated civil rights slogans. After a while she turned around, and she and her own seatmate began chatting about other things.

The sun was beating into the bus on all sides—even though it was January, the temperature outside was about seventy degrees. By then we were near the hot, truck-packed exits—the Thirties—but this didn't stop her from happily telling her seatmate that she had ordered up some Chinese food for lunch before the trip, and that her husband was a judge. Ordering up Chinese food on a warm afternoon before a long bus ride was a real mistake. Then I imagined a sixty-five-year-old judge, probably a corrupt Housing Court judge, in his black robes downtown in his chambers with all the other corrupt judges. The judge's wife and her seatmate were becoming best friends, even though the seatmate was a rich-looking white woman, about five foot ten, wearing black toreador pants, ballet slippers, and eight or ten bracelets. As her bracelets clinked together she confessed that she had been a cruise-ship attendant—it sounded like a confession—and she had married an airline executive and they had a little boy, who'd been born when they lived in Senegal. When asked about the obstetrical care in Senegalese hospitals, she said, "It was fine. They have you hang from a tree by your wrists." I began to feel ill when I heard this, even though I knew that the use of gravity was better than the American method of lying on a table. It was the picture of the former cruise-ship attendant in labor, hanging by her wrists from a tree—this picture plus the combination of the heat, the fumes, and the idea of the Chinese lunch ordered by the woman married to the judge presiding downtown in Housing Court. The Mozart in my earphones couldn't help me transcend this.

Every now and then the former cruise-ship attendant would laugh with inappropriate abandon. I decided that she was drunk. In order to distract myself, I made a plan to ask Dr. Loquesto about the technique of childbirth she'd described, but on second thought I realized that it might enrage him. I'd once heard him yell at someone who asked his opinion of the birthing chair, "Great, the doctor has to sit on the floor in a raincoat!" Everything seemed worse when I remembered this incident.

It was another muggy January day at the midtown location that same winter when I concluded that I would never ride the South Fork Bus again. It was Thursday afternoon and I was aiming for the bus that left East Seventy-third Street at one o'clock. Because of some kind of demonstration, there was the most miserable kind of thick, slow traffic on the way up Park Avenue. The taxi driver suggested we go to the midtown stop. I said O.K., although I had a fear of midtown, and then we agreed that the only thing demonstrations ever accomplished was traffic.

I asked the midtown commandant where to get some coffee, even though I wanted tea—I was afraid he'd say, "Tea?"—and he pointed me to a hellhole combination stationery-and-coffee shop. In the hellhole I saw midtown individuals of every wretched sort, and stuffed animals of the poorest quality made. But in the back, behind every other kind of thing a midtown person would want—for example, a cheap kind of foldup umbrella, a lavender rabbit, and the most dreaded candies and magazines known to man—there was a little Indian clerk whose job was dispensing coffee and tea. I was amazed to see a selection of herbal teas on a shelf behind him. I ordered a peppermint tea and a black coffee. I thought, I'll try the tea; if it doesn't help me feel any better, I'll try the coffee; if it makes me feel worse, I'll switch back to the tea.

Behind my small canvas bag in the line for the South Fork Bus, fifteen more people had arrived during the ten minutes I was gone. These passengers were stunned to see a long line on a January afternoon. A former debutante was behind me. She said that once it was so crowded she had to ask to sit next to someone. "I asked if I could sit there and the person said, 'No.' "

"What reason did the person give?" I asked.

"No reason," she said. "Just 'no.' It took me a long time to get over that incident."

"I'd never get over it," I said, remembering the three-hundred-pound man I saw once. No one asked to sit next to him, and after a while you had to feel sorry for him, since his great girth was obviously the reason. But as he settled into the trip and discovered that he knew the couple in front of him and began to tell them about his new life in Water Mill, you had to hate him. Because in his new life, although he was around fifty-five, he and his new wife had a one-year-old son named Jake, Josh, or Zack, and his wife and son watched the sun rise each day before she went for her three-mile run on the beach. A very typical description, I thought, as I heard him say his house was right on the beach and then ask the couple where their house was. They said their house was right on the highway. Now, that was a surprise. He didn't know what to say to that. This was as embarrassing to hear as hearing a couple say that their son was a pornography star or a follower of the Reverend Moon. There was nothing to say in reply. The couple didn't seem to mind that their house was on the highway. They took it lightly; it was the same house they'd had all these years. Maybe the highway wasn't so busy twenty years ago. Still, that was no excuse, and the couple and the three-hundred-pound man all knew it.

That trip, starting with the demonstration and the debutante, was the end for me. I got on the bus, alternately sipping my tea and coffee, but neither one was helping. The seventh seat on the right was taken by what looked like a purple sweatshirt with a tough-looking woman inside. It was going to have to be the eighth, closer to the center accordion divider of the bus. This was the new, extra-large bus, which appeared to be two pieces of a bus joined together by a flimsy vinyl connector. In a crash, the back section would fly off and smash into everything—cars, trucks, trees. The front, at least, would still be steered by the driver, this time an angry-looking, red-faced thug who would have a seizure because of his physical condition, which I diagnosed as high blood pressure and arteriosclerosis.

The debutante sat in the front with a friend who had gotten on uptown. Very quickly, I saw that someone was going to ask to sit next to me, because the new passengers, to their dismay, were having to sit with other passengers all over the bus. First they'd walk through the front section and through the accordion to the back, thinking that there certainly would be empty seats in the back. Then they'd come dejectedly back down the aisle and survey the choices. In front of me, in the seventh seat, a woman—the purple sweatshirt—with badly dyed hair was asked by a man if the seat was taken. I couldn't tell what she said, but he walked to the back. I was studying what had gone wrong with the hair-dyeing process when a man came by and asked me if the seat next to mine was taken. I had to tell the truth, because if you lied to a decent specimen, a worse one would be coming by next. I should be flattered that this man has chosen me, I thought, because this man was perfect as men go. He was (1) clean—clean as a man can be. His hair was clean, his blue jeans were clean, his boots were clean, his cotton socks were clean, his skin was clean, and, as an added bonus, it was perfect skin, too. (2) He was only about forty. (3) He was wearing a wedding ring. (4) He had a book.

He wasn't going to bother me.

Across the aisle from the purple sweatshirt, a most elegant man had sat down next to an elderly lady. The elegant man wore a perfect, lightweight gray pin-striped suit; a blue-striped shirt; and a blue-striped tie. I wondered how the elegant man had just the right weight suit for this warm winter's day. He was an investment banker, I was sure, because these bankers have all the right clothes no matter what else is wrong with them. One thing wrong with this man was his face. His face was too small, his features were too small for a man's face, but what could he do? He was a man. He couldn't get out of it. He wore black shoes—a mark against him—but at least they didn't have gold buckles. His hair was too long for his profession, and it was thin on top, but he didn't let this bother him, and he bravely combed it back the way he'd always combed it. He had a suntan on his small-featured face, but not too much of a suntan, and his hands were tan and smooth-looking, as if he'd never done anything with them but handle financial papers and cut a twig in his garden. This man was going to get off at Southampton. I imagined him in prep school. I imagined his whole privi-leged life of about forty-nine years and how he might have managed to keep his hands like that. Servants hammered and sawed things for him in Southampton, and superintendents and porters helped with things at home on Park Avenue.

Before we had even taken off I saw that the elegant man was talking in a cordial way to the purple sweatshirt. What could he have to say to her? He wasn't looking directly at her when I heard him say, "I keep mine out on the East End." I realized that he was smiling warmly at her dog, her dog that was the reason no one sat with her—her dog sat in the win-dow seat, although dogs were not allowed on the South Fork Bus. He spoke directly to the dog, and, to my astonishment, he called the dog "pooch." "Hi, pooch," I believe he said. I couldn't tell what kind of dog it was. It looked a bit like the elegant man himself, with little tiny features on its little tiny face, but its face was a squashed, flat, light-brown fur thing, and his was not. The dog had big ears surrounding its tiny, bashed-in fur face, and the man's ears were normal-sized.

I saw that my seatmate was listening to his Walkman, a newer and more expensive model than mine, and that he was reading his book. There was no way to see what he was read-ing, but I saw that his hands were not only clean, they were beautiful. The more I stared at his hands, the more grateful I felt to have him sitting there. His long legs in those tight, but not too tight, clean, naturally faded blue jeans were not only good legs, they were great legs, but his hands were perfect hands, and suddenly I had the urge to grab one and kiss it.

Once we were out of the tunnel, I noticed that across the aisle the elegant man and the purple sweatshirt were exchanging newspapers—he had *The Wall Street Journal,* and she had the *Times.* They were friends now, just because of this dog. They were smiling at each other with each exchange of sections, and there were seven sections altogether. If they were in a Mozart opera, they might get up and dance a minuet. How could he like her so much just because she had this dog? It didn't seem possible, because he was so elegant and she was a slob. He'd smile his courtly smile and she'd smile glowingly back even though she couldn't have been interested in him, since she was so tough, and he was some kind of neuter man.

By the time we reached Manorville, I noticed that the elegant man had stopped reading. He was becoming fidgety. When he saw that the bus was stopping at Manorville he got nervous. He mentioned to his seatmate, the elderly lady, that this was really too much, to have to stop at Manorville—the trip was taking four hours instead of two, the traffic was terrible, and now all these new stops.

Soon after Manorville he started to bite his nails. But he didn't manage to bite them. He would start, and then think better of it. Just a small nibble starting at the index finger and going across all the way. Then he began to run his hands through his hair. He'd run his hands through, and then he'd stop, and start to bite those nails again, but he never got into it. The hair, next the nails, and then he began with his ears. Rubbing his finger around the rim of his ear madly and almost poking it into the center. Then he'd look out the window and squirm around in his seat and start on his nails again. At one point he started to take a big chomp out of all four fingers at once but reconsidered and stopped.

This elegant man is going to go crazy on this bus, I realized, and I had those few Xanax with me. This is what they were for, but I couldn't offer, and he would never ask. I became afraid of what would happen if he continued this way to Southampton. But he did continue. Look out the window, I tried to direct him by mental telepathy, which I didn't believe in. Look out at the beautiful country view, look at the landscape. See the sky, see the fields, see the trees, calm down, you are almost at your destination. But he wouldn't calm down. The hair-running, the brink of nail-biting, the ear-rubbing; and then he added nose-rubbing to it—a quick flick across each side of that tiny Pekinese nose was added to the routine. There was nothing left for him to do but put his face into his palms and rub his eyebrows and forehead upward in a final act of desperation—and then he did that, too.

I'm not going to watch anymore, I decided, even though the best view was out his window. I tried looking out the window next to my seatmate and saw to my alarm that the clean, beautiful-hand man was writing inside the cover of his book. I had no trouble seeing that he was keeping a diary, a moment-by-moment diary of his trip on the South Fork Bus. "3:04. This f—— bus!" it said. I looked at another section and saw that he was also writing about some failed relationship. I hoped it was not with a man. It appeared to be about his innermost feelings, feelings that I thought men didn't wish to express, but here he was expressing them in a diary.

When I saw a sentence that began, "So many feelings," I decided not to read on.

If I closed my eyes and concentrated on the sonata in my Walkman, either one of these two passengers could go berserk and I wouldn't see in time to escape. Neither one was calming down. The sweatshirt and her dog were asleep. The diarist put away the book and started taking deep breaths. I decided to speak. "We're not even at Southampton," I said to him, "and it's four o'clock."

"It's always late," he said, as if he might start to cry. "I hate this bus. At least . . . the train . . . I can walk around."

"Do the windows open?" I asked.

"No, but you can go to the end of the car and get some air," he said.

Finally, at Southampton, the elegant man turned calm and polite; he was helping the elderly lady on with her coat. People knew him. They were all getting off together, shaking their heads in disgust.

"Where are you getting off?" I asked the diarist.

"East Hampton," he said. "I can walk home. I live on Further Lane."

I could see that he was used to having people gasp when he said the name of his street, because this clean, half-crazed man lived on the most beautiful and expensive lane in East Hampton. The elegant, more crazed man must have lived on the most beautiful lane in Southampton—Pond Lane, or one of those Neck Lane roads.

Even though it had started to rain by the time we got to East Hampton, I knew that these two men would change their clothes and go out running. I couldn't run, but I could walk so fast it would be just as good for the heart.

On my walk I'd try to think of a new means of transportation. I'd heard that people hired retired policemen to drive them back and forth. It was only two times the price of the bus. I knew a man who had gone to police school but flunked out because the police hat he'd purchased was too large and kept falling over his eyes, and his shoes were too small to chase criminals in. Maybe his rates would be lower.

I could get a part-time job to pay the flunked-out police trainee his cut-rate price. I had no skills for the real world and didn't know anyone gainfully employed except for the flower arranger and a macrobiotic chef. I could work arranging flowers by day and cooking brown rice at night. If only I'd shared those Xanax with the flower arranger, but drugs had become so hard to get. Dr. Loquesto had recently given me a prescription for one Demerol for a medical test. And the flower arranger had told me that his dog knocked over a bottle containing his last few pills and then tried to lick them up. The flower arranger had to scramble around the floor trying to salvage the licked pills for himself.

I'd always listened attentively to his floral techniques. "First, I mossed up the table, then I strewed calla lilies in wet Oasis—you know, the green foam Oasis?—then I draped ivy. . . ." While we worked on bouquets, we could talk about flowers and pills and herbal remedies. The medium-strength Xanax was a pale-peach color, the same shade as the Apricot Beauty tulip we both admired. The mild strength was white, like a White Emperor tulip. An even higher strength than the peach was light purple, my haircutter, Francine, had told me. "They're for extreme cases," she said. I pictured a lilac and a freesia. Valerian root could induce calm and sleep. Echinacea drops had antibiotic properties and came from the coneflower.

I'd have to hear the word "moss" turned into a verb. Dr. Loquesto said he didn't mind hearing the word "laser" conjugated as a verb. In my new job I wouldn't have the authority to say " 'Moss' is not a verb." Still, if I could learn to moss up tables and strew calla lilies in wet Oasis, maybe I could earn enough to hire the flunked-out police trainee with the big hat to drive me back and forth. That was my plan.

A Lovely Day

The sun was getting ready for the summer solstice, but I had made a plan to photograph seven doctors with their dogs, and the first doctor and his dog were set for a date that turned out to be the hottest day of June.

It had taken me months to work my way up to this photograph. First I had to be cured, so that I no longer needed the services of the first doctor, Dr. Arnold Loquesto, the world-renowned reproductive surgeon. Then I had to photograph him in his academic office, next in his clinical office, then in the hospital corridor carrying his worn-out briefcase. Then I had to photograph the dog alone, and, finally, the supreme photograph—the surgeon and his dog together.

When the idea first came to me, I was nearing the end of my time as a patient but had not yet been dismissed. I told him about my plan, and asked, "Can we talk about the photograph now, or should we wait until I'm cured?"

"Wait till you're cured," the surgeon said. Then he shouted, "Right now you have me fused with your uterus."

Once I was cured, I noticed that the goal of reproduction had receded into the background and had been replaced by the goal of taking photographs of the surgeon, especially the surgeon and his dog. I had first encountered the dog when the doctor agreed to allow me to photograph a group of reproductive surgeons who were gathering for a dinner meeting at his house. I thought this subject matter would be entertaining and fascinating for various reasons. Although he'd seen some of my photographs, the best ones didn't interest him. "I'm too busy for surrealism," he yelled as he walked down the hall. "But take any photograph you want. A photographer once came to take a picture of a tree we have." Unfortunately, while the cure was dragging on and the busy surgeon was racing around the world to medical conferences, the short winter days were getting longer and the long hot days of summer were forcing their way in.

Even in March I knew the sun was starting to interfere with everyone's plans, because one muggy warm day I found I needed the car air conditioner on the way out of New York to East Hampton, but it was out of Freon. I attempted to live in East Hampton all winter but couldn't because of my husband's profession. "I can't be a dean at Southampton U.," he'd say. Only a university in a filthy, decaying city was right for his line of work, dean of the school of architecture. The man I had hired to drive was wearing what looked like an all-polyester blue-and-pink plaid shirt, and he had the sleeves rolled up. The shirt fabric wouldn't crease; it looked like something spun out of those tubes of plastic that children used to use with a straw to blow bubbles. In the heat and the traffic my driver tried to keep a stiff upper lip—in fact, his facial expression was always the clench-jawed, hollow-cheeked look of the FBI man he had been.

I knew this driver's whole life story and the life stories of all the other drivers I'd had to hire to drive me out of New York. My own driving experiences and my witnessing a fist-fight on the South Fork Bus made the driving service a necessity. I knew that the driver had learned to stop drinking milk while at FBI school, that he had changed all his eating habits during that time, and that his wife had "taken this opportunity to lose forty pounds." I knew that he and his "whole family enjoyed stir-frying in a wok." This sounded like good news until he told me the ingredients he liked to stir-fry: beef, pork, and two omelettes cut into tiny pieces, all to be stuffed into spring rolls.

This was a big part of my life, sitting in the back seat of our fifteen-year-old Volvo station wagon with my camera case, my photographs, and my Walkman and the *Trout* Quintet. The *Trout* Quintet was the only piece of music I could stand anymore for the trip, and I was on my way to not being able to stand that, either. I'd sit and listen to these ingredients and these life stories as we went up the incline of the Long Island Expressway toward the orange-and-white gas tanks. Even on the tree-filled Northern State Parkway the driver's wok recipes sounded sickening, but, certainly, anything would sound worse on that stretch of road to the tanks.

To rid my mind of thoughts about heat, plastic, and the consumption of animal products, one warm January day I had decided to start the project of photographing the seven doctors and their dogs. My photographs of flowers in every stage of decline were "not what most people want to see," a gallery owner had told me the week before.

But when I saw the reproductive surgeon Dr. Arnold Loquesto, at home with his dog, I knew that this was something everyone in the world would want to see. If not everyone in the world, then a few people in a few cities and towns. No, all doctors and patients would have to be interested because a photograph of a doctor with his dog—especially this doctor and his dog—would show what no other kind of photograph of doctors showed. I had the idea that the way these doctors looked at their dogs would reveal what I was trying to discover—either the evil in their natures, or the kindness, or both the evil and the kindness.

No one could tell me how Dr. Loquesto had come to his position of power. Some people didn't want to discuss the subject and just shrugged. They had probably suffered under his reign of terror. Everyone tried to follow his orders, everyone feared him, and the medical staff at the great Massachusetts hospital and medical school where he ruled all trembled with fright when his thundering footsteps announced his arrival at the clinic. He had the deepest, loudest voice I'd ever heard. Immediately I pictured him as King Lear, though his style was great comedy, not tragedy. Many actors struggled and trained throughout their careers to have the booming voice of Dr. Loquesto, a voice that could be thrown across long corridors through the closed doors of examining rooms and operating rooms, and could wake patients from light or even medium anesthesia as he operated on them. His fame could be attributed as much to the things he had shouted as to his surgical skills. Once, during a medical test, he warned me, "If you're going to get nauseated I'm leaving, because that's one thing I can't stand."

But with his dog everything was different. His little wild dog would jump up on the humans in the dining room, as well as on the surgeon himself, and the surgeon would order the dog to get down, but the dog would ignore him. Everyone followed the surgeon's orders except his dog, and the surgeon didn't mind.

At home, as I discovered when I attended that first dinner meeting of the reproductive surgeons, his dog jumped around and did whatever he pleased, leaping at the doctor's wife, scampering about, biting his leash, biting my wrist at one point, and jumping onto people's plates. The doctors gathered in the surgeon's study for the buffet dinner didn't see the comical aspects of the relationship, and proceeded with their discussion of some dull statistic. Once, during the evening, when the surgeon was taking a handful of popcorn, even though he had just eaten dinner and dessert, as the dog jumped up with his paws on the surgeon's chest he appeared to be almost as tall as the doctor, though the doctor was of average height and the dog was very small.

As I tried to schedule the photograph of Dr. Loquesto and his dog I began to worry that the dog would grow beyond this stage of behavior by the time the surgeon was free for the photography session. Because when his three secretaries read me his schedule for February and March—the last good months before the hot weather began—I saw that the doctor was too busy for me to ask for time for the appointment. All of his secretaries had different versions of his schedule, which they were glad to rattle off: "He's here the fourth, he's away the sixth, he's back the seventh, he has surgery the eighth, he flies to Brazil in the afternoon, he's back the tenth for one day."

I remembered the panic caused by hearing these schedules when I was still a patient of the powerful surgeon. Because what if you needed him? He was never there. "I'm here today," he'd say enthusiastically when the subject came up. "I leave my number, wherever I am." And this was true—when he was traveling you could call him at 9 P.M. and hear the sound of a TV program in the background. What could the lonely surgeon be watching in his first-class hotel room? "I stay in some seedy third-rate hotels," the surgeon told me when I asked about the accommodations on his trips. That was something I didn't want to picture. Also what he was watching on television was something I didn't want to know. It didn't sound like the news. I knew if I asked he would tell me. "I hate Harold Pinter!" he yelled when I said I liked *The Birthday Party*. That was the generous part of his personality— he'd tell you anything, no matter how badly it reflected upon his character.

I could see from the surgeon's calendar that there would be no time for my plan until June. I pictured the dog's growth from March to June, and it worried me. I knew the dog would be different. I thought about the six other doctors and their dogs. Some of these dogs were not that young. A dog could die of old age, or be run down in the road. A doctor might have to replace his dog with another pet. I might arrive to find a doctor alone with a parakeet. One of the doctors himself might die. That wouldn't be as bad. Because only a few of these doctors were great men; several were hateful, if not evil men. Maybe the photographs would show that there were no great men left in medicine.

I knew nothing about the growth patterns of dogs. I did know that a kitten could get to be a cat in a few months. I had just watched my neighbor's kitten turn into a cat in this way. Suddenly, one day as she was holding the animal, I noticed that the cat was a giant, its body spilling out over and under her arms, fur everywhere. I realized how quickly the cat had grown, and I immediately thought of Dr. Loquesto's dog. Oh, no, I thought, that little dog is growing, too!

It was during the moments when Dr. Loquesto's secretaries were reading me his schedule that I reevaluated my ideas about time. They read so fast I couldn't even write the dates down. "Here . . . away . . . here . . . away . . ." And that was how the months flew by—he was here, he was away. It was March it was April it was May.

Whichever thing the doctor was doing at any moment, he was always wanting to get on to the next thing. Once, I asked him, "What's the ultimate thing you're always in such a hurry to get to?"

"Well," he answered straightforwardly, "first we have the meeting, then we have the discussion, then we have the dinner."

"I mean what's the ultimate goal?"

"Ultimate goal? There is no ultimate goal. I have to keep moving."

There was no ultimate goal, after all. I'd noticed this before—that those who were not going insane just kept moving. People were calm as they went about their daily rounds of wrong choices and futile pursuits. But I saw that moments could become separated from the activities that were supposed to take place during the moments. I could see a moment coming and I could feel a moment passing and I could see all the moments that had already passed. Every moment lived in the present was on its way to being the past. In this way I understood that all moments were nothing and didn't really exist.

The sunlight at certain afternoon angles showed moments to be more dead and empty than they were on a cloudy day. On a cloudy day, the moments of afternoon could merge into one long moment, but on a sunny day you had to be on guard and watch what the light was doing to the time. The way the sun was shining into our garage and lighting up an old pink silk chair made it seem to me that we were already dead. My husband's woodworking projects had the look of a man's work when the man has just tragically died. The sun was lighting the front of the birdhouse he'd been shingling, and even though he was just out running and I was taking a photograph in the garden, our things had that feeling of the dead.

If you were to keep on moving instead of staring at the reflections and angles of sunlight, maybe you could be as happy as the surgeon.

By the time June arrived—June, that dreaded month with the approach to the summer solstice—I had a new driver for the trip. This driver was younger than the other drivers and wasn't encumbered with a house or family or mortgage to talk about. He loved to drive, he said, no matter how long a trip I was planning. He'd be willing to drive from Southampton, where he lived, and take three ferries to New London and drive to the surgeon's hospital in Massachusetts and back, or he'd drive from Southampton and even pick me up in New York first if I was there for a dental appointment. He'd be willing to drive us to Mt. Desert Island or Nova Scotia

when we left for the real summer in search of a more northern climate.

He was so young he was from the generation of human
beings who use the word "like" to mean "said." "I'm, like,
'You've got to be kidding' " was one of his expressions.

"What are these malls supposed to look like?" I'd ask him.

"That's just it," he'd answer, and he'd answer that to
almost anything.

"The Expressway may be more direct," I'd say. "But there
are all those trucks."

"That's just it," he'd say.

"If they're working on the Merritt and the Taconic and on
I-Ninety-five, how are you supposed to get to Massachusetts?"

"Exactly," he'd say. "They don't care."

As the day approached for the important appointment, I
studied the weather reports on all the television channels and
saw that it was going to get hot all of a sudden. Some of the
more stupid weathermen would call it beautiful when a day
like that burst in upon the days of normal weather we
remembered from the past. Beautiful somewhere else, but not
in a city; they never explained that, and there was no way to
contradict them, because there was no editorial reply to the
weather report.

Only one weatherman denounced the heat and loved snow
and cold weather. He loved blizzards. I imagined a life with
this weatherman, but he was overweight and getting bald all
over his head at once, although he was just forty-two. I could
tell he ate lamb chops and peas and that he was some kind of
philosophical conservative. In any case, I realized I couldn't be
married to him, but still wished we could be friends.

My new driver was overweight, too. I was shocked to meet him and see his extremely chubby face. Luckily, on long drives I didn't have to see his face and think about his diet but saw only the back of his head. The new, chubby-faced driver hadn't figured out how to turn on the air conditioner during his broiling three-hour drive from Southampton to New York City, and his large round face was all red. In addition to this he was wearing a sweater. At least it was cotton. "Weren't you hot?" was all I could think of asking him.

"Like I said, it wasn't too bad," he said.

"Like I said" was one of his favorite expressions, although he often used it when it didn't apply, since he hadn't said anything yet. "Exactly," "Like I said," and "That's just it"—with these three expressions he didn't have to elaborate on anything.

The hottest June day arrived on the same day as the appointment for the important photograph. By then I knew the driver's life story and all the fun things he did in his carefree, low-pressured life. "We're just going for a bite at the Golden Dragon," he would say on the phone, and it made me wish to be going along to the Golden Dragon with them, although I knew it was a bad restaurant, maybe the worst in Southampton.

Why did I have this crazy day ahead of me when I could have low-achievement goals, relax, and have fun the way other people did? I saw the usual ten thousand cars on the F.D.R. Drive, but for some reason they were headed south. Thousands wanted to enter New York City on this blazing-hot and humid June day. Who were they, and what were their reasons?

"Now are we takin' the Taconic, the Merritt, or the Inter-state?" the driver was going to ask at any moment, and whichever I chose would be wrong.

I had brought along some changes of clothing. I'd wear a thin linen shirt, and if the day turned out to be one of those killer blasts of hot air, I'd change into a thinner one. I'd wear thin cotton kneesocks from Switzerland, and I could change into thinner cotton anklets from Italy. Then I'd leave my dis-carded clothes on the back seat in a bag while the driver drove off and waited at a friend's house in some hot suburb. My plan was to meet the surgeon at his academic office in the hospital, take a few photographs, then go to his house and photograph him with the dog.

We weren't even across the Connecticut state line when I'd changed into my lightest shirt and socks. Why couldn't the surgeon stop working so hard in the hot weather? It was hot where he lived, near the Berkshires, but he didn't realize it yet, because in his youth, at summer camp, the Berkshires were still cool. "When is your vacation?" I asked once. "Never!" he shouted.

When I arrived at two o'clock, the surgeon was sitting at his desk, blowing his nose. "That selfish jackass doctor!" I was privileged to hear him yell in his academic office. "Can you believe it? He keeps statues on his air vents! He blocks the whole air system so it's freezing in here! I have to endure bit-ter cold temperatures for years!"

"He probably doesn't have room for all his things," I said. "He doesn't know the consequences."

"Right—he doesn't have room for his things," he said hatefully.

"You should be glad that they can get it so cold here. In New York they can't get it cold enough."

"I'm not glad! I had a cold yesterday and it got worse from the cold air."

"It couldn't have gotten worse from cold air. You just felt worse."

"That's right. That's what a cold is. You feel worse."

"What is a cold?" I asked.

"A virus," he said.

"If you were on a macrobiotic diet you'd never get a cold. I read in George Ohsawa's book that even one cold in ten years is a very bad thing."

"I don't want to hear about it. Take your macrobiotic books away. I'm not interested."

"You could eat brown rice every day."

"Rice? I ate rice—let's see—I ate rice last week."

Then this was the surgeon's philosophy. He'd do whatever he pleased. " 'You are what you eat'—Camus," he once shouted at me. He'd ignore all the medical articles about nutrition and health, articles that appeared weekly in the Science section of the *Times*—he'd have already ignored the original articles in the *New England Journal of Medicine*. He'd gain weight, he'd get terrible colds, he'd blow his nose and keep throwing Kleenex into his large wastebasket, which would be overflowing with papers and boxes, and topped off with mounds of used Kleenex—and this wouldn't bother him. You knew doctors had bad health habits, right, but you didn't know that surgeons sat beside large wastebaskets of used Kleenex right in their hospital offices, and that they didn't mind that no rubber-gloved, masked hospital employees came around to empty the baskets. If I made a study of the personality of the happy-go-lucky reproductive surgeon—and the way to do this would be to photograph him with his little dog—I would have the answer to the question of how to live in the world.

I decided to photograph the two shady corners of the office, even though there was nothing in the corners but books and other inanimate objects. I'd put these photographs together in a way that showed the surgeon's surroundings, and in this way the picture would be complete. I was surprised to see through the camera lens that I was photographing a photograph of the surgeon's parents and children. "Does this little boy still look like this?" I asked.

"You'll see when you get there," he said mysteriously.

I asked if I could photograph the clinical office. He said, "Yes, come over there with me now. Then I have a meeting at four. You can't photograph that. Meet me back there at five." Then he dashed from the room.

After photographing the examining rooms in the weird fluorescent light, I decided to go outside to buy some bottled water. I walked a few seconds into the jungle heat and turned back. I could feel my light linen appearance disintegrating.

The surgeon wasn't in his clinical office at five o'clock, so I drank some of the warm bottled water I found in my briefcase. An overweight resident who looked like an appliance repairman appeared. At least his trousers weren't slipping down. He said Dr. Loquesto was waiting in his other office. When I got there, I saw that his lab coat was thrown onto a chair and he was dressed in his real clothes—a gray suit a businessman would wear and an ordinary striped tie. He appeared to have just combed his wavy light hair so neatly that he'd acquired a new glued-down look. This must have been what was meant in macrobiotic philosophy by "the contradictions of the universe." So intelligent, yet this hairdo.

As he led me through the blazing heat of the parking lot, I realized that he would have to unlock his car door so I could get in, and this would leave him with the decision whether to open the door, which would be completely against his nature, or leave it closed after unlocking it, and this would be ruder than his nature. He unlocked the door, then opened it with a kind of miserable resentment.

"Are you going to turn on the air conditioner?" I asked after I got into the car.

"I never use it!" he shouted.

"Even on the highway?"

"We're not going on a highway."

"But do you, on the highway?"

"Hardly ever. That's not fresh air either that you get from an air conditioner."

"But it's cool air. You could leave the windows open a little and have both."

"Never!" he shouted. "I'd never do that."

If only I had planned things so that my driver had picked me up and driven me to the surgeon's house and dog. But I felt I should take this chance to be driven by the surgeon himself, in order to see the angle of his profile in his tiny black Ferrari. His driving style would give me information I could use, if it didn't cause the kind of accident that kills the person in the passenger seat. He'd already told me he enjoyed speeding. Maybe he would try to control himself with another person in the car.

Being trapped in that hot little car with the demonic surgeon at the wheel felt more dangerous than being operated on by him. At least during the surgery some strong sedative was dripped into my veins, preventing panic at the idea of what was going on. But in his car there was no sedation. I guess I could have said, "Please let me out here," on the side of some dusty road, but that would have destroyed the semblance of the normal personality I was cultivating to help me complete my project.

Before we were even out of the city part of the town I had to adjust the sun visor. But wherever I moved it, the sun was everywhere else. The surgeon was using one of his hands to block the sun from his eyes, because he wasn't wearing sunglasses. He was going to drive into the sun, speeding for thirty minutes without sunglasses or air-conditioning. He was a madman. I tried to put my hands behind my neck and stretch my elbows out, so I could get some more air into my lungs, but there was no room for my elbows—they were going to hit the roof of the car or the edge of the surgeon's ear. I unfolded my arms and sat with my hands clenched in my lap. The surgeon sped fiendishly through the gusts of hot air, and soon we were in a suburb that looked as if it had been a forest some developers had destroyed in the nineteen-sixties.

All of a sudden we were in his driveway and then in the hot dark garage. The surgeon jumped out of the car and raced in through the door to the kitchen. But I couldn't figure out how to unlatch the seat belt, and had to sit in the tiny car in the sweltering garage and work on it. It would be a real imposition on the man's personality if I had to ask him how to unlatch the seat belt. From this trapped position I peered through the doorway into the house.

Inside the kitchen I could see there was a hot, empty silence. The surgeon forced his way into the hot emptiness of his kitchen as if he didn't notice it and yelled this normal sentence to one of his children: "Is Mom home yet?"

Into the stillness of the empty kitchen a boy came out of nowhere and said, "Not yet." Then he disappeared. Did the surgeon know that if his wife were to leave him this empty stillness and silence would be what he would come home to?

I managed to get out of the car and followed the doctor through his nineteen-fifties-style kitchen. Different boys appeared from different passageways. I guessed their ages to be from ten to fourteen. It had to be a hundred degrees in the house, but no windows were open. The boys didn't seem to mind the hundred-degree temperature in their home and walked in and out of rooms as if it were sixty-eight or seventy.

The doctor sat down to read his mail.

Although I'd been in this house with these boys before, the doctor had never introduced them, and I didn't know if it would be O.K. to speak to one or two of them.

"What's it like out on that porch?" I finally asked a boy who appeared to be about ten. "Is it any cooler?"

"You can try, but it's hot there, too," he said.

So they all just sat in their hot kitchen and never even ventured onto their porch, which was so rarely used that it was locked. There was no porch furniture anywhere. As I opened the storm door, I saw that the little boy was right. It was just as bad, but the air wasn't as old as the air in the house.

Only the dog seemed to mind the climate. He was lying exhausted in a corner of the kitchen floor. Because of the day's weather and the surgeon's behavior, I'd almost forgotten the purpose of my trip. I had to look at the dog and assess his development. The outline of the dog on the floor seemed to be two inches larger than it had been a few months before. Maybe he had gained a pound, but he was the same gray color as the linoleum, so it wasn't clear what was the dog and what was the floor. Surely the doctor's wife would come home and throw open the windows and turn on a fan in a fit of common sense. Then the dog might jump up. This was all I could hope for—and that she would come home soon.

Obviously the surgeon was the kind of man who never opened a window or hammered a nail in his life. If he had, then just on principle he'd never do it in his own home, I could tell. He was used to having things done for him, and like the upper classes in the Arab world, as I'd once heard, he found menial labor beneath him, although he wasn't any part Arab. But he might as well have been an Arab, since he had his own set of rules for behavior which no one understood. There are experts to explain the behavior and customs of the Arab world. For example, I'd heard on CNN that it's an insult to an Arab to show the sole of the foot when one is wading across a river. But the surgeon's hospital and medical school didn't have an expert to explain his behavior or how to act in his presence. On the same day, one doctor told me, "He has a good heart," and another said, "He has no heart."

This has to be the worst project I've ever gotten myself into, I thought as I tried to make my way back through the thick, heavy airlessness of the kitchen. The surgeon was still sitting at the table. A view of the kitchen cabinets would be his only view if he chose to look up while reading his mail. But he chose not to look up. He methodically went through his mail, dispensing with this or that piece and yelling "All right!" and "O.K.!" every minute or two. I don't even open my mail. I thought about my unopened mail as I watched the surgeon.

There were many things I could learn from the surgeon, other than the subject of his expertise, reproductive surgery—which he refused to talk about even when or especially when I was his patient. His rule was to use one word as an explanation when ten words were necessary. A grunt of agreement was preferable to a whole word, and his favorite word was "No!" shouted as loud as he could, or "Wrong!" If you were wrong in surmising something when he refused to give an explanation, he liked to say "Yes." When he said "Yes" this way his face looked like a rubber mask that someone has just taken off and hung on a hook somewhere. Just rubber without a person behind it. I had never seen this look on the face of a human, but thought I remembered it on the face of an animal Julia Child was about to do something to. So much was going on in the man's brain that the only look he could get into his eyes was the look of an animal that had been dead and refrigerated for several days and now lay on a marble countertop. He had mastered this trick in his battle against communication.

Once, I asked him, "How did you survive the feminist era?" He said, "Huh? Survive? What do you mean, survive? I'm a supporter of women, I'm very good to women. In this profession . . . I help women training to be in this profession."

"You help women the way people help dogs they're training to do tricks," I said.

"That's help. What's wrong with that?" he said.

As the surgeon proceeded with the reading of his mail, his four sons and their two friends wandered in and out of the kitchen and glanced at him. I hadn't yet figured out which were the sons and which were the friends, because they all looked alike except for the youngest boy. Maybe because of the heat they had no energy to act like boys, or because they looked alike the older ones all seemed to be the same boy. Five boys melded into one; the heat and the sticky conditions blurred the lines of distinction among them, the way the tigers in *Little Black Sambo* all ran around so fast that they melted. These boys had melted into something like pancake batter and poured in and out through the doorways into the kitchen from time to time. This had to be the greenhouse effect getting under way.

The little boy and his brothers, when glancing at the surgeon at work on his mail, would smile the way people smile at the antics of a comedian they like to watch. Yet he was engrossed in his tedious chore and ignored what went on around him. He never asked to have a window opened or to have a fan turned on. I didn't see any fans. He didn't get himself a glass of iced tea. And then he shouted, "O.K.!" and jumped up from the table. "I'm going to watch the news," he yelled.

"After the news, do you think you might be ready for the photograph?" I asked.

"We'll see. First do the dog. One thing at a time," he said. Then he disappeared into the television-watching room.

I asked the youngest boy if we could go outside. He took the dog's leash and attached it to the dog's collar and opened the front door.

It was the hour of the day when mosquitoes like to come out, although the sun wasn't making any progress in going down. Every time I looked at the sky and at my watch, that monster was still up there. It was maybe an eighth of an inch lower. I knew that when the sun finally moved down, the heat was going to hang about this suburb even after dark. And after walking around the wooded area that was the backyard, searching for a site for a photograph of the dog, I realized that I didn't have the best lens for the dim light that was descending upon the woods. Mosquitoes were buzzing around the boy and were taking bites out of his arms every few seconds.

"Are there ticks around here?" I asked.

"We have a high rate of Lyme disease," he said matter-of-factly. I showed him a suspicious rash on my ankle but he wasn't impressed. I could tell that nothing would impress this boy.

He led me back to the house, which seemed to have gotten even hotter. Does prolonged exposure to heat and humidity affect perception, I wondered, as I stood in front of the TV room. There was the surgeon, lying in a semi-prone position, leaning on his hand, watching the news in color on a big TV screen. There were several giant-sized TVs in the room. They were all on the same channel, and the colors of the newscasters—their wardrobes and their faces and their hair and the maps behind them—were orange and turquoise and bright pink. The room didn't seem to be a real room, with all that glass of the TV screens around, and in the fluorescent glare of these colors it seemed to be more of a tremendous aquarium—only the air bubbles were missing—and the semi-prone surgeon floating above the upholstered rocky cove appeared to be a large underwater creature, like a dolphin. I felt that I was watching a rare specimen in its captive habitat. The colors of everything in the room seemed to have joined the colors of the television screens and were all moving around the dolphinlike doctor in waves.

The surgeon looked up at us in the doorway, and I noticed that his glasses were the same style as the ones they put on dolphins in advertisements for a real aquarium in Mystic, Connecticut, which is always being criticized for exploiting dolphins for their good nature and high intelligence. I knew that even in the same glasses the doctor was not as good-natured as a dolphin and was less communicative, too.

I ventured to ask him, in his transformed state, "Do you want to see the tape I brought of Michio Kushi talking about grains?"

"No," he said. "I'm watching the news."

"Oh," I said as I backed out of the doorway to the aquarium. "O.K."

The youngest boy was heading toward the kitchen. He was supposed to put a casserole in the oven, but he didn't know what the right temperature was. The other boys guessed different temperatures, all of which I knew were too high. Although it wasn't my place, I thought I could suggest the right temperature. "Two-fifty is high enough," I said.

I saw that the thing being heated wasn't anything people should eat but something like meat loaf, and I was participating in its heating up. I supposed the surgeon had eaten meat the night before operating on me when I was his patient, but what could I do about that? I supposed that meat eating went on in every segment of society including health-care and medical professionals, but it would be best not to think about this now. The boy was putting on some red-and-white polka-dotted pot-holder mitts, without any under-standing of how they looked. He looked at them seriously as he put them on his small hands, as if skill and precision were necessary to put on these simple mitts. I hoped this little boy wouldn't be following in his father's footsteps. I hoped he would be some kind of chef instead of some kind of doctor. Time didn't stand still. This boy was going to grow up along with his dog. Probably he'd have another dog before he went to college. He might go to medical school, though I hoped not, and his mother probably hoped not, too. The boy would grow up, and this day nearing the summer solstice, this year just past the prime of my life, would be only a memory to him. "This photographer once came to take a picture of my father and our dog. Boy, was she weird!" That could be the whole thing.

Suddenly the surgeon appeared out of nowhere. He seemed to have crawled through a tunnel to the kitchen like a mole or a groundhog to get some food. Because first he was in the aquarium and then he was up on his feet in his kitchen ready for dinner.

"Did you get a picture of the dog? I wasn't in the mood to have my picture taken before," he said.

"The light wasn't right for the dog," I said.

A jar of something called Butter Buds appeared on the table.

"I've never seen this product in real life," I said.

"What's wrong with it?" the doctor asked.

"The ingredients. All fake."

"Good, good, we love that kind of thing," he said.

Soon the surgeon and the boys were eating the hot meal in their muggy kitchen and I was gathering up my photography equipment.

"Did you ask our guest if she'd like a plate of string beans?" the doctor asked the youngest boy. "Do you know you have to call her Mizzzz?"

"Can't he call me by my first name? I'm not a librarian in 1954," I said.

"Then you'd be Miss. Or you'd have to be Mrs.! Ha!" the surgeon shouted.

"Do you want any string beans?" the boy asked.

"Maybe she wants something to drink," the doctor said to the boy.

"How about something like Pellegrino?" I asked.

"We only drink soda—diet soda," the doctor said.

"I have some water in my briefcase. You know, in my childhood my father forbade any soda products in our home."

"Why?" the boy asked. From my position in the living room I heard the doctor muttering "It figures" and "No wonder" while I was digging around for my bottle of water.

This room felt even hotter than the kitchen. I was forced to catch a glimpse of myself in a large gold-framed mirror. My light-pink linen shirt was creased all over, and there was a line of dark-blue ink down the front. I didn't care whether it would ever come out at that point. Because I saw no future beyond this second for myself in the shirt—I saw only this one moment of ruin. Obviously, I shouldn't go out into the world. I should stay with flowers in gardens. My socks had rolled down around my ankles, and my pleated linen skirt had unpleated. Long pieces of my hair were going every which way, like a caramel spun-sugar decoration I saw Martha Stewart demonstrate on David Letterman's show while he paid no attention and tried to make fun of her.

As I took a sip of my warm water, I heard the surgeon say with relief, "It's Mom!" A few times during his dinner I'd heard him say, "Mom must be having a good time in New York," as he looked sadly at the door he hoped she would walk through shortly.

The surgeon's wife had come home, although she could have run away for good. Not only had she spent the whole day in New York City, but now she was smiling at everyone. She had the permanent smile of a doll I had saved in its original box since I was five. Maybe she was just shell-shocked from her years of living with the surgeon's personality. It had to be a shell-shocked smile, or the smile of the Stepford wives. These wives, I recalled, had the rebellious part of their brains destroyed in order to make them the perfect domestic creatures men wanted them to be.

The whole family cheered up when she came home. How lucky the doctor was! She looked as if it were a bright new morning with clear blue skies and no humidity. She was wearing dress-up, grown-up clothes—a white silk shirt with long sleeves that weren't wrinkled or rolled up. She had on a triple strand of pearls, though women who owned such pearls told me they never wore them in hot weather, because they would cling in their hot, pearl-like way to their necks. The skirt of her suit was the narrow kind you can't walk in, but she said, "We walked all over Madison Avenue." She wore stockings and high-heeled shoes, and in these things she had walked all over the place I was always trying to leave. She wore some gold bracelets I couldn't identify, but I knew they were a really good kind, in demand by women of the Upper East Side. Instead of running upstairs to tear off all these things, she sat down and began to tell about her day in New York. Although we're about the same age, she looked twenty-seven or nineteen.

"You mean you walked all around Madison Avenue in high heels?" I said.

"I'm used to high heels for work," she said, smiling. "I love to go to New York and walk around. I might lose some weight."

"Even in June?" I said. "Everyone I know wants to leave."

"You live there. That's why." She smiled again.

"We all hate it," I said, speaking for the entire city.

"Hot weather doesn't bother me. Was it hot here? I did take my jacket off," she said, smiling.

"You drove yourself all that way on the highway?" I said.

"I always do. There was traffic this morning, but it wasn't too bad."

"We must have passed each other on the F.D.R. Drive," I said.

"Maybe," she said, still smiling. "Didn't you have anything to eat?" she asked me with a look of concern.

"She doesn't eat anything we have," the doctor said.

"We have apples. Would you like an apple?"

"I ate a peach this afternoon," I said.

"It's some macrobiotic thing," the doctor said.

"Not to eat more than one fruit a day," I explained. "Only three a week, I think."

"Why?" she asked.

"Too yin," I said.

"What's that?" the boy asked.

"Yin and yang," the doctor said with disdain.

"For example, he's too yang," I said, "and I'm too yin."

"She only eats brown rice and seaweed," the doctor explained.

"It's too hot to eat anyway," I said, going back to the dining room.

I knew I had to remove myself from the midst of this happy, normal family, normal even with the surgeon as a part of it. My film was on their dining-room table with some contact sheets. I didn't want to get these things mixed up with their chandeliers and vases. I decided I'd come back for the major photograph in November, if it cooled off. I hoped the dog wasn't due for a big growth spurt.

I could still hear the doctor's doll-faced wife talking about her day in those high heels. "We had lunch at the museum, and then we looked at Oriental rugs," she said.

If only they were cotton rugs, I thought. If she would just take off her jewelry and change her shoes. But she was sitting there the way ambassadors' wives are trained to sit and seem comfortable at teas and receptions.

The surgeon was pretending to be listening. I guessed he was so happy she had returned that he was trying to seem interested.

"Really, we had a lovely day," she was saying again. "Just a lovely day." I saw that she was smiling again. And I had to wonder exactly what did she mean. In what way was it lovely? I knew I'd have to discuss it with my driver.

"All the windows were closed," I told him. "No one minded."

"Where I was, too. They said, 'It will be hotter if you open them'!"

"What?"

"I know! I'm like, 'It will?' "

"But we live near the ocean. It's different. These unfortunate people live inland."

"That's just it. At least did you get your photo?"

"No, the doctor had a cold and the dog was too hot. But what do you think she meant by 'lovely'?"

"You know, I don't know."

"How could it be a lovely day? What does she mean?"

THAT'S NO FUN

We were on our way to have dinner with our friends who lived in the woods. They didn't live out in the woods—just raw woods—the way elves do, they lived in a house in the woods of Southampton.

"You know I hate the woods," I had to say to my husband whenever he tried to get me to walk in various woods with him. He'd ask, "How can you hate woods if you love nature?" and I'd explain, "I like light, open fields and wild moors, not dark, closed woods." My husband had resentfully compiled a list of wooded places I had refused to walk in over the years. "The pine forest in Nantucket, the woods all over Maine, Nova Scotia, France, and Italy." Just as he had compiled a list of movies I'd prevented him from seeing after movies had gotten to be so bad. "When the Oscars are announced, I haven't seen any of the movies," he complained to an intellectual filmmaker who was our friend. "You're lucky," the filmmaker said to him, and then looked at me with admiration.

My husband had such a poor memory for other things, but as for these wooded areas, he was able to remember every one and list them bitterly whenever the subject came up. He said he didn't want to walk alone in the woods. He'd say, "You would love it so much if you would just try it." He'd promise that we would come across rare birds and flowers.

There were times when he had tricked me into walking in the woods by promising that there was only a short wooded area that led to a wide-open space—the water and the sky. On one of these walks I pointed out a man wearing a camouflage outfit and carrying a bow and arrow in a case. "Look," I said, "a hunter with a weapon."

"It's not a weapon," my husband said. "It's some kind of binocular equipment."

"What about the camouflage?"

"He doesn't want to frighten away the birds he's trying to see."

The second one of these guys we passed had his bow and arrow out of his binocular case.

"What are you hunting?" I asked him in a friendly way.

"Deer," he said. "But they're getting away."

"Is it safe for us to be walking here?"

"We're pretty well sure of our target before we shoot," he said with a big grin.

I had seen deer hunters like these on the news explaining how they happened to kill this or that person walking nearby.

"They're way over there," he said, pointing to a spot a few feet away from where we were standing.

This would be a good way for my husband to get rid of me, I thought as we left the forest that day. But no matter how many woods I had kept him from walking in, it couldn't be reason enough to hire a hunter for murder.

On this night, preparing to visit our friends in the woods, I had offered to bring a few things for the dinner. I'd done this for two reasons. One: It was the au pair girl's day off. That meant our friends had spent the whole day alone with their four babies, all boys under five, and they would be too worn-out to cook. Two: Even when they were in the right mood to cook, they cooked inedible things. The wife of the couple was Swedish and she had Swedish ideas of what to eat. Once, this is what was spread out on the table: a platter of meatballs, gravlax, five cheeses—a few were the kind with mold—hard-boiled eggs, butter, bread, and sliced pickles. Finally I had to eat a piece of bread and some pickles, but this was out of politeness, not hunger.

The mother of the Swedish wife was visiting, and during the so-called meal she got up and made an omelette as her contribution to the dinner. She must have felt she had to do something, because she spoke no English and couldn't do anything but smile agreeably when the conversation around her wasn't in Swedish. Sometimes her daughter would explain something to her in Swedish and she would smile and say "Ya."

This was O.K. with me—I could sit back all night and hear them talk Swedish to each other without understanding a word. But some words were almost the same as English words, and I almost understood them. For example, *klocka* had to mean "clock." These words were like parodies of English and reminded me of an actual parody of an Ingmar Bergman film, or of all his films. It was pleasant for me to listen to these conversations translated into Swedish, and after a while I'd feel that I could float outside the conversation and not have to be part of it. Whatever they were saying sounded so much better in Swedish than in English.

When I first saw this meal of all animal fat and animal protein I remembered hearing that in Denmark this is what people ate. A friend had told me that the Danish people she saw everywhere on her visit to Scandinavia all had rosy cheeks and high blood pressure from their diet of butter, cheese, and meat. Although I hadn't heard this about the Swedish people, ignorance of Scandinavia, as well as of most other parts of the world, led to my lumping countries all together in regard to their dietary preferences. I knew that the Swedes liked to commit suicide, and if this was their diet, maybe it was the reason.

If our friends, this couple, ever prepared a vegetable, it would be a nightshade vegetable on a macrobiotic list of "Never Eat"; for example, eggplant, peppers, potatoes, or tomatoes. They soaked these vegetables in oil, usually Bertolli olive oil from a plastic bottle, and then they grilled them. As a variation from the nightshades they might serve asparagus, from the "Avoid" list. They were all screwed up in this way, and so was their refrigerator. Almost everything in there was in a plastic bottle. Everything else was in a plastic wrapper— chicken, meat, and cheese would come tumbling forth from every shelf when I opened the door to look for some Perrier. But there never was any Perrier, and only once was there Pellegrino. Their two-year-old boy sat on my lap that time and said, "More Pellegrino, please," every few minutes. This was the only time I got any Pellegrino—when I shared a glass with this baby boy. Other times I'd have to go to our car in their wooded driveway and get my own bottle of water from the back seat. "Sorry, we have no water for you," they'd say, "but we forget you don't drink wine."

This time I had offered to bring the salad, and when I pictured their olive oil I made some salad dressing, too. When I remembered the nightshade vegetables I offered to cook broccoli a way it was served in an Italian restaurant where the chef pretended to be from Tuscany, although he came from Brooklyn.

While I was washing the leaves of three kinds of lettuce and steaming the broccoli, my husband sat in his chair watching television and switching around to all the channels in his favorite pursuit—seeing what else is on. Although he knows how much I hate the sound of this activity, he keeps on doing it. He really began to get on my nerves when he got up and stood at the door doing nothing while I tried to put all the food into shopping bags with a bunch of white tulips I had decided to bring. "Maybe you could help me carry some of this," I said.

One reason I was afraid to visit the couple was their children. We might feel bad when we saw them because we hadn't managed to have a child yet, or we might feel good because these half-Swedish babies were especially adorable, but then that would quickly make us feel bad again. One boy was a baby and still seemed surprised to have been born. He had a big red face, as big as a balloon, with black hair sticking out in all directions. Sometimes I'd try to rearrange his hair, and when I told him how it looked he'd laugh. "Now it's like Tom Snyder," I'd tell him.

Part of his charm was that he'd laugh at everything. "Doesn't he look like a fat old lady in a housedress in the

Ozarks?" I asked on one visit. The baby's parents took this to
be a compliment, which it certainly was. His eyes were such
a light blue that he had a really Christian look, as if his ancestors had run after and thrown rocks at Jews, although I knew
this was impossible because he was Swedish, not Polish, and
the Swedes were so tolerant of minorities and so perfect in
every way. Mai Britt had married Sammy Davis, Jr. That was
an example often given of Swedish liberalism, I recalled, or
maybe not—it was an example of something, I couldn't
remember what, as I looked at the baby's light-blue eyes and
tried to picture his ancestors. His name happened to be
Christian, too—a choice I couldn't understand, because his
father was half Jewish, and it was almost like being named
Jesus.

It would have been better to name him Tubby. My husband had a list of nicknames he said he wished he'd been
called. On his list were: Butch, Chick, Jumbo, Slim, Slick,
and Jinx. In my childhood I'd known a boy named Tubby—
not a very nice boy. At a birthday party for his little sister,
Irma—he was nine at the time—he'd done a magic trick, and
the trick involved something like putting pepper on a hand-
kerchief, which caused one of my older sisters to sneeze. My
sister couldn't forgive Tubby for this, saying that it wasn't
funny, or magic, and that it was dangerous to cause sneezing
fits in others. We all had allergies, and later on we developed
cat asthma, a condition not taken seriously by most people
but acknowledged by Dr. Arnold Loquesto, the world-
renowned reproductive surgeon I'd consulted and photographed, when I removed a cat from my chair at a dinner
party. "Cat asthma!" he shouted enthusiastically. "We'll have
to perform an emergency tracheotomy!"

"Here, use this," I said, handing him a silver letter opener someone had just given the hostess as a house gift. "Here— use this!" was my favorite line of dialogue from a movie, ever since I'd seen Loretta Young say it to Orson Welles, in the film *The Stranger,* when she discovers that he's Franz Kindler, the Nazi monster she has unknowingly married. She hands him a fire tool to use to kill her. "When you kill me, don't put your hands on me!" she says. "Here—use this!"

When I first looked at the baby, Christian, I wondered how Tubby had liked his name. His parents owned a run-down boatyard next to a creek and they lived in a white stucco house with red trim. It looked like a house on a Christmas card and not in the real world. His father was known as "old man Reilly," and his mother looked like a worn-out Peggy Wood in the TV program "I Remember Mama."

The other thing I was afraid of—in addition to the food and the children—was that there would be no real dinner-time conversation. I tried to remember what a conversation was. What is a conversation was something I wondered when we were dining with certain people, almost all people. The last true conversation I'd had was with Dr. Loquesto's eleven-year-old son. He had an opinion about everything that came up—usually a low opinion.

But the half-Swedish couple didn't have ideas about subjects that came up. Subjects came and went. What was it like when we weren't there—with their more compatible friends? Once or twice we were there with these friends, but because we were there, too, it put a damper on everything. The dinner passed as a blurred long moment. At the end of the last course a male guest got up from his seat, picked up a whole pint of ice cream, and ate it all in a few big spoonfuls. And I hadn't seen or smelled marijuana being smoked.

I didn't know what a conversation was anymore, just as I didn't know what a tomato was anymore. I'd see one and I'd want it. Then I'd cut into it, and when I saw those seeds and that juice I'd think, "What is a tomato? Does anyone really know?" Then I'd eat it anyway.

In the car on the way to the woods, I held the tulips in one hand and the salad dressing in the other. We drove in silence down the dismal road. "We hate where our house is," the couple would often say. "We like our house but we hate getting there." They'd given me a new idea for my work—to film people in their houses telling what they didn't like about them.

"You have to pass the dump," the Swedish wife would say whenever the subject came up. Since they had to pass the dump, they could have gone in and recycled all their plastic bottles. But they didn't. The one advantage of proximity to the dump was overlooked by the couple, who bought every product available in plastic and then tossed the empty bottles into a plastic bag filled with good garbage that should have gone into a compost heap, which they didn't have. Another advantage of living in the woods—ease of keeping a compost heap hidden somewhere behind a pine tree.

The last place I had seen carbonated beverages in giant-size plastic bottles was in the refrigerator of the reproductive surgeon, Dr. Loquesto, and I had never got over this sight. Now, I knew that the couple never read the *Times* and didn't watch CNN. The doctor always read the *Times* and watched all the news, and when he missed articles about toxins in the food supply, I sent them to him. Because the doctor was in his forties, he had a basic education that could be added to. But the husband and wife were in their thirties and had to be completely educated whenever anything came up.

It was getting more and more difficult to be friends with couples under forty. Some of these people owned no books. Others didn't care about Mozart or Elvis Presley. When I saw the couple's new house completed—they had designed it and had it built and had actually chosen the woods for the site—I saw that there were no bookshelves. I said, "Where will the bookshelves go?" The husband looked startled, not because he'd forgotten about shelves in his building plan but because he realized they had no books.

"That's O.K.," he said, calming himself quickly. "We'll find a place."

He knew how to be calm and secure, because he had once taken a course (in California, naturally) that taught people how to be whatever they already were—I *think,* because usually I lost consciousness when he explained what the course was about. It sounded close to a Scientology or est course I'd heard described by some course survivors on a television program about these things. The husband's ability to remain calm was one of the reasons we became friends with him—a bad reason, on second thought. Because we'd tell him something like this: "The temperature of the earth has gone up four degrees in this decade." And he'd say, "Hey, no big deal, we'll all get central air-conditioning."

The last time we knew some couples born in the decade after ours, I saw that they were in a whole society of couples who spoke this way. When the men greeted each other in the street or in a restaurant they'd say, "Hey, what's happening?" and the answer was usually "Hey," because what could be happening? These men would grin in genuine happiness at seeing each other—there was a bond of emptiness between them.

I thought these things over as we drove through the woods. I felt silly holding that bottle of salad dressing and those white tulips. I had made the dressing in a bottle I'd saved from Israeli tomato juice. Although I knew that tomatoes were from an extremely yin nightshade plant, I still had the desire for them. I had a lingering fear of Israeli tomatoes and oranges, having once heard that Arab terrorists threatened to inject them with cyanide, but I was in the mood to live dangerously the day I bought that juice.

I had also brought along my house shoes, because in Sweden, as well as in Japan, people took off their outside shoes and put on their inside shoes before entering the house. I thought this was an excellent custom, and my husband said he thought so, too, but at our house he preferred to walk right in wearing his sneakers. I was able to sling the straps of my indoor shoes over my fingers and carry the shopping bags of food and flowers at the same time. What was my husband planning to carry? A sack of wine would be his addition to any dinner. I knew that he and our host would soon be slugging some down. Our hostess, too.

The husband and wife were sitting together in a corner of their dark living room and didn't get up to let us in. Their three-year-old boy came to the door when he heard us open it. He said something in Swedish before taking the tulips and running over to his mother.

"Why does he speak to me in Swedish?" I asked. "I never know what he's saying."

"He thinks all women speak Swedish," the husband said. "You look more Swedish than his mother does," he added, looking at his black-haired, brown-eyed wife.

"No, she looks more Finnish," the wife said, giving me a critical glance.

The boy came back and put a big book in front of my face. "Look, my new book—read it," he said.

I was preparing myself for a dull children's book when I saw that I was looking at something beautiful. Not only that, but the words on the cover were Swedish and I didn't have to know what they meant. In the picture were what looked like giant-sized blueberry trees with butterflies flying and bees buzzing around them. The blue of the blueberries was bluer than a real blueberry, and the the trees and the leaves were a soft green, not the deep, dark green of a real forest.

"What is this beautiful book?" I asked.

"It's Swedish—it's mine from my childhood," the wife said, pronouncing it "shildhood." "Isn't it wonderful?"

And I remembered quickly that everything in Sweden was wonderful, and that this was going to be another opportunity to hear about it. But this was fine with me. I was as patriotic as the next person, the kind of patriot who doesn't mind hearing how much better things are in Scandinavia. But if things are so great in Sweden, I always wondered, what are all these Swedish women doing here? Sometimes I'd ask this question. The answer was something vague like "It's more interesting" or "There's no future in Sweden."

Under the blueberry trees, which appeared to be the size of apple trees, there were two perfect spiderwebs, and inside each web was a spider. On both sides of each tree there was a large bumblebee, and above one bee, near the berries, there was a big, pale-golden butterfly.

"Who illustrated this book—van Gogh?" I asked.

"No, the writer illustrated it. Isn't it wonderful?"

The little boy was standing at my side trying to open the book. I was staring at the blue of the berries as I heard the two husbands and the wife plan the start of the drinking. They were discussing which wine to begin with. These two men had spent a year trying to buy a winery in California, and when the plan fell through they ended up just drinking a lot of wine.

I wished I could get inside the picture underneath the big blueberry trees.

"Read," the boy said.

"O.K.," I said, "but I don't read Swedish. A boy is walking through a forest. It's so beautiful—it's in Sweden, not the kind we're in now."

"That's right," his mother said, laughing. "In Sweden the forests are so beautiful. They're not just woods."

"For some reason the boy is sitting on a tree stump crying as he talks to a tiny elf," I said.

"Why is he crying?" the boy asked.

"I don't know, because I can't understand any of the words."

I turned to the next page, where an animal looking like something in between a squirrel and a rabbit had a blueberry basket on its back.

"What's that?" the boy asked.

"The ears are too long for a squirrel. What is this animal?" I asked his mother.

"It's—how do you say?—it's—you know—a squirrel. But it's the kind we have only in Sweden—this beautiful, light-brown—like a deer—not gray like here. They're so cute, with these big ears. I think it's a squirrel—no—yes, a squirrel."

For a minute I thought she was going to come up with another kind of animal, but this was just as good—a better kind of squirrel. The boy had run off and was riding around the room on a little plastic tricycle.

"Come back," I said. "The boy and the elf are in the forest now."

I decided to read on alone. Soon, little boys, dressed in blueberry costumes, were in a field of blueberry trees in front of a thatched hut.

The corks were popping and the wine tasting had begun. The wife was in on it and seemed too tired to get up for the hors d'oeuvres. I saw that she had regained her figure and was wearing tight blue jeans and a black turtleneck sweater. The husband was wearing black slacks and a black sweater, too.

"You're both in black," I said.

"Yeah, well, we're idiots," the husband said.

"It's the Roy Orbison look," my husband said.

"We didn't plan it—it just happened," the husband said. "And you're both in beige," he added.

"You have a black Saab," I said.

"That was a real mistake," he said. "I couldn't wait for a good color. But, hey, you have a beige Volvo."

The blueberry boys had climbed into the trees and were pulling down berries and throwing them into one boy's blue cap.

The husband was talking about some power tool, and soon they'd be discussing how big a hole to dig for a certain size post.

"I just can't understand what's happening in this story," I said to the wife.

"See," she said, finally getting up and coming over to explain the pictures in the book, "The boy is crying because he's sent into the woods to find blueberries and he can't find any."

"Who's this elf?"

"That's the Blueberry Father, and he comes to help the boy. He shrinks the boy down so they can go into the blueberry bushes. Here the boy is all shrunk down in the forest, and these are the Blueberry Boys. See the little blue hats? They're dressed as blueberries, and they're sailing in this shell from a nut."

"Oh, now I see. That's why everything is so big. What is this beautiful red fruit?"

"Those are lingonberries," she said, leaning over and smiling. "This is the Lingonberry Mother. She has with her the Lingonberry Girls, and the Blueberry Father has the boys."

"This was before the feminist era," I said.

"This book is so old—you know. They have these lingonberries in Sweden, fresh lingonberries with cream—they're so delicious, just picked in the season."

The word "lingonberry" sounded especially good in this Swedish accent. Lingonberry.

"This is the most beautiful book I've ever seen," I said, thinking I sounded drunk, though the real drunkards were soberly talking business.

"You see, then the Blueberry Boys and the Lingonberry Girls all meet in the forest with the little boy, and they eat the berries at this picnic."

This wasn't the way my mother or father read stories to me. They were never drunk, they didn't wear blue jeans, they didn't wear black to read fairy tales.

If I were this lucky Swedish woman I could never leave a country where an author had produced such a work of art, a country where people sat in fields and ate blueberries and lingonberries out of wooden bowls.

"I have more books by this author," she said, handing me one. On the cover there was a picture of some tiny boys in round, red caps climbing on what looked like a mold-covered rock. But inside the book I saw that the boys were in a field of man-size mushrooms. "Giant mushrooms," I said. "The writer is preoccupied with one theme."

"These are the little mushroom boys—they're from a mushroom family who live in the mushroom woods. This was my favorite book."

"Are there any homeless people and filthy streets in Sweden?" I said.

"No, we don't have anything like that there. In the countryside people do these things—they pick mushrooms and berries and have picnics."

"I see a girl flying through the air on a little bat—that's going too far," I said, closing the book. "One thing I can't face is the idea of a bat."

"In Sweden the bats are different. They're not big and black and scary."

"Do they have rabies in Sweden?"

"I never heard of it in modern times."

"Why don't we all live over there?" I said to everyone.

"We always ask you to come with us," the wife said.

"If I weren't afraid of airplanes I'd go to the Salzburg Festival," I said. "I'd like to fly over on one of those pleasant little Swedish bats you have."

"I'm ready to take a plane," my husband said.

"Hey," the other husband said.

They picked up their wineglasses and toasted the idea. They would toast any idea.

Soon we were all in the modern Scandinavian kitchen trying to do a few things. The husband started to throw some asparagus into a pan of water. "Wait—I haven't washed them yet," I said.

"Wash them?" he said. "Hey, good idea. But you don't eat asparagus anyway, right?"

"I don't want my friends to eat DDT."

"Hey, alcohol kills things," he said.

"Alcohol doesn't kill pesticides," I said.

"It must kill some things," he said.

"It kills humans," I said.

"For thousands of years man has drunk wine," my husband said drunkenly.

" 'Alcohol is a toxic drug, harder than heroin'—I just read that," I said.

"Don't quote from that Michio Kushi book," my husband said.

"No, this is from a doctor who graduated from Harvard Medical School. You can believe someone like that."

"I do believe it," my husband said, taking a big gulp of wine.

"Wouldn't you like anything to drink?" the wife asked me. "I'm sorry we have no Perrier again." She bent down to search in a cabinet and came up saying, "Here, I want you to have this," the way someone gives away a precious family heirloom. In her hand was a small jar of sliced pickles.

"My favorite food," I said.

"They're Swedish, from Ikea. We got the shrimp there, too."

"Oh, no—I forgot to defrost the shrimp," the husband said. "Oh, well, I'll make spaghetti. Everyone loves tomato sauce."

"What kind of pickles are they?" I asked as I tried to read the Swedish ingredients.

"Normal pickles—how do you say it?" the wife said. "Taste them, they're delicious."

"If I taste one, I might have to eat them all."

"And you're not even pregnant," she said.

"What are these Swedish shrimp like?" I asked. I wanted to know, because every time shrimp were mentioned, the wife said that she ate shrimp only in Sweden.

"I can't describe it," she answered. "Once people have them, they can never want to have shrimp here."

"You mean shellfish are cleaner in Sweden?" I said.

"Of course they are," she said. "The rivers are clear and blue."

"Shrimp are from the ocean, I thought," the husband said.

"The oceans are cleaner, too," she said.

"You mean they don't dump everything into the ocean? What kind of water-treatment program do they have?" I said.

In my childhood, when I envisioned the life of a grown-up, I never thought that I would grow up to ask the question "What kind of water-treatment program do they have in Sweden?" To me, an example of things grown-ups did was this: One night when my parents went to the theater in New York, my mother wore a black taffeta dress and a tiny black sequined hat. When she came home she said that she had met the actress Ruby Dee, and Ruby Dee had admired her hat, so she took it off and gave it to her. Whenever I see Ruby Dee I wonder whether she still has my mother's hat.

Eventually the dinner was on the table. The table had been set in advance, unlike our table, where things are thrown on at the last moment. The diners quickly became engaged in a conversation about their wines of the evening.

"A nice Chablis," the husband said.

"A great Chablis," my husband said. I never heard such loud swallowing.

"Very fine," the other one said, swishing some around in his mouth like mouthwash.

Soon the wife joined in with some compliments of her own. "It is good," she said with a dazed look.

Then they started a bottle of red wine. The cat jumped up onto a chair next to mine and looked right into my eyes. I picked up a spoon and touched the fur with it. "I can't touch you," I said to the cat.

"Get him to move," the wife said. "Come here, Ingmar," she called. The cat jumped up into her lap.

"I like his company," I said. "Even though he wants to kill and eat birds."

"I eat birds, too," the wife said in her accent.

"You don't pounce on them and kill them in your garden."

"You know I love to eat little ducks," she said.

"It must be hard for you to be a macrobiotic vegetarian," her husband said to me.

Suddenly I noticed that no one was eating the salad or the Tuscan broccoli. Instead, they were eating creamed potatoes and some gravlax that had been added to the meal to make up for the shrimp.

"This is a typical Swedish meal," the wife said. "Creamed potatoes and gravlax."

"Have some salad," I said. "I made the dressing the way the Tuscan chef told me to."

"What's his secret?" the husband asked.

"Two secrets for everything," I said. "One is olive oil, the other is garlic. I used only half the olive oil, because that chef weighs three hundred pounds."

"Where's the other half of the oil?" my husband asked.

"Here," the other husband said, passing the saucer of olive oil. "You can put some on the gravlax."

"Why don't you pour it over everything?" I asked.

"Oops," the husband said. "I spilled a little on the chair."

"But my deerskin shirt is on that chair!" the wife said. "This is my best thing that I brought back from Sweden!"

"What's it doing on the chair?" her husband asked.

"I had no time today to pick up everything. Look, big stains of oil," she said, holding up her shirt. "There's no way to clean suede of something like this."

"This is your chance to give up wearing animal skin," I said.

"I eat it, I wear it," she said.

"We can cook the shirt and eat it," the husband said.

"I married this person?" the wife said.

"I bet there's some special Swedish method of cleaning it," I said.

"This could never happen in Sweden," the wife said with sorrow.

"What a beautiful tablecloth," I said, hoping to cheer up my friend. "Is it Swedish?"

"Yes, I brought it back with me. I'm bringing my beautiful dowry—is that how you call it?—into our home where olive oil is spilled on my best suede clothing."

" 'Never marry for love,' my mother said," I said. " 'Money lasts but love doesn't.' This was her motto, but she figured it out too late."

"Kind of a cynical motto," the husband said.

"Her mother was cynical," my husband said.

"But she gave her hat to Ruby Dee," I said.

"Why did I ever get married?" the wife asked the cat as she looked into its eyes. "Even you, you're a man-cat. I live with all men, why did I do this to my life?"

I saw that she had taken on a new, sultry quality I had never noticed before—she sounded like Marlene Dietrich in *Shanghai Express.*

"I'm going to make coffee and tea," the husband said. The two men walked into the kitchen in a spirit of camaraderie.

"They're going in there to encourage each other with their bad behavior," I said when they were gone. "We hear your drunken muttering," I called in to them.

"Why did I get married?" the wife said wretchedly. "I should have been a lesbian."

"No you shouldn't have!" I said. I was surprised.

"Could you open the cabinet and bring out the chocolate?" she asked me, pronouncing it "shocolate." She was slumped down in misery but still had enough sense to want the drug chocolate is known to contain.

"Which do you want—the little candies or the giant bar?"

"Both," she said. "And could you get a sjar?"

"You don't mean this?" I asked, showing her a plain storage jar her husband had handed me. "You mean a bowl?"

"Yes, any bowl."

"Where did you get all this Swedish chocolate?" I asked.

"Ikea," she said, unwrapping one of the little candies and putting the red wrapper into her empty wineglass.

My husband seemed to have suffered the most ill effects from the wine. When the evening began he looked something like Cary Grant, but as he drank more I caught him looking like Rodney Dangerfield. His eyelids were swollen, as if bees had stung them. His face had melted together and didn't seem to be his original face.

"Well, I guess you can't always understand the things your wife wants you to," the husband said in a summation of something, I couldn't tell what. I hadn't heard a discussion or anything that could be summed up.

"This is why women have to eat pickles and chocolates," I said to my dinner companions.

"Why?" my husband asked.

"Before I go back to Sweden I'll have to go to the sgym and do sit-ups," the wife said, looking at the wineglass filling up with red chocolate wrappers. "If we're killed in a plane crash, would you adopt our children?"

"We'll be killed on the Expressway first," I said.

"But we always fly to Sweden," she said.

"Then the whole family will be killed," her husband said reassuringly.

Soon the evening would end. I could look forward to the next day and another medical test in the laboratory of Dr. Loquesto. "By the way, when you had your cesarean, did you have Demerol?" I asked the wife.

"Yes, in my veins, it was so wonderful. I was like, 'Give me more of that!' "

"Do you know whether Demerol pills work?"

"Yes, when they took away the I.V., I had pills. Why?"

"I have to have one of those tests tomorrow where they shoot dye through the tubes and take an X ray. But I'm sure I don't have blocked tubes."

"Then why is your doctor doing the test?"

"He says he can't take my word for it. He'll be disappointed if they're not blocked."

"Why?"

"He loves to unblock tubes surgically."

"That's no fun."

"He says it's fun for him. Your doctor loves to do cesareans. They all have their favorite things."

"It was worth it for my four beautiful boys."

"He said he'd get me the fun radiologist," I said.

"Fun how?" she asked.

I thought about the surgeon and in what way the radiologist might be fun. I made a plan to bring my Discman and two Mozart piano sonatas. Maybe I'd even bring *The Magic*

Flute, or *The Marriage of Figaro,* which I had just purchased on three different recordings. I could take a Demerol, and a Xanax, too.

Some sort of conversation seemed to be starting again. Although the words were English, and I understand English, I couldn't tell what the conversation was about. It had to do with lumber. Moving lumber around.

I tried to think of something pleasant, in a foreign language—like a Mozart opera. I saw a view of the future. I'd become an "all-Mozart opera lover." I'd go to meetings of friends of alcohol-dependent persons. The mother of a man we knew joined Alcoholics Anonymous and liked it so much that she joined Schizophrenics Anonymous even though she wasn't a schizophrenic.

Maybe I could somehow get to the Salzburg Festival and go to a different opera each night, or, even better, go to the same ones over and over. I could photograph the musicians; we often find that great musicians and opera stars are plump. I could photograph them with their food supply and show them the road to macrobiotics. While engaged in this new project, I could find out what was on Schubert's mind when he wrote the *Trout* Quintet, and whether it was Mozart who really wrote it. Because how did Schubert all of a sudden get so happy? I thought about these plans, and then I thought of the Demerol and the Mozart and the doctor's disappointment at finding normal tubes. And I thought that except for his disappointment, hey, it might be fun.

Were the Ornaments Lovely?

When people ask me what I did for the holidays I tell them the truth, but they don't believe it. Because in the weeks before Christmas I go to the Discount Drugs store to look at the decorations and products necessary to celebrate the holidays, and I go to the East Hampton A&P to hear Christmas carols piped through the store on their loudspeakers. I feel lucky that I have these two places to go. When we lived in New York City, there was no place to go for this kind of celebration.

Discount Drugs deserves the award for preparations for holiday festivities—once they kick things off with Halloween. It's a long wait through the six-month summer we have now until the shelves of orange candies and plastic masks finally appear. Between Easter and Halloween, it's a bleak time at Discount Drugs. It's that bleak time now—May—with the empty summer months ahead.

During the months of long daylight we should avoid going inside stores lit with fluorescent bulbs. It's a waste of your life and a crime against nature. It's best to wait until dark to enter, and this isn't easy in June, because the drugstore closes at eight-thirty, just when it's getting dark out.

Every Discount Drugs store must have its display up by a certain date. I learned the schedule this year when I asked the manager, "Why do you have the Valentine hearts out when it's only January 2?"

"We have to have them by December 27th," he told me. "It's an order from headquarters."

"Beautiful," I said, staring at the big, dark-red cellophane heart boxes of candy.

"Thank you," the manager said. "It's all my work."

"You did a great job," I said. "Except it might be better with all hearts and no stuffed animals."

"We don't control what's in it," he said. "It's all directed from headquarters."

Under the red cellophane there was a brighter-red satin, and I remembered that my mother had been given a red satin heart box by my father when I was seven. My mother wasn't happy with the gift, because she wanted to avoid candy-eating, and the candies were an inferior type. Some were filled with light-green jelly. During the same era my father also gave her a Christmas present of a maroon nylon quilted bathrobe from Sears, Roebuck. She didn't like that, either. But she kept it, unlike Jacqueline Kennedy, who, I'd read, returned a red cashmere sweater she'd received for Christmas from her husband the President.

I started my close relationship with the manager of Discount Drugs a few years ago, when I couldn't find Clorox in its usual place. "They did away with the Clorox," he said. "We don't know why."

"They can't," I said. "People need it." I remembered hearing Rex Reed say that whenever he interviewed Marlene Dietrich she was scrubbing the bathroom with Clorox.

"It's done from headquarters, there's nothing we can do about it," the manager said. "Also glue—we have no more, and it's not going to be reinstated."

During a reorganization of shelf space a few weeks later, the bottles of bleach reappeared. "I see the Clorox is back," I said to the manager. I was really happy.

"Yes. And did you see that we got our glue aisle again," he said with pride.

Even though my arms were filled with half-gallon jugs of bleach and I didn't need any glue, I thought I should at least visit the glue aisle, the way I had to see Michelangelo's David when I was in Florence, even though I was having an attack of not being able to take a deep breath after seeing too many people at an exhibit.

There was definitely something wrong with the employees of the drugstore. One of them was such a mess that when he was working at the cash register I'd try to figure out how to buy the items I'd chosen without having him touch them. The man was about forty. He was bald on top of his head except for one tuft of blond hair that stood up and went out in a few directions. The band of remaining hair growing around his head stuck out and flew up all around, too. I hated it when I had to ask this man a question. The man had never encountered an instructor of yoga breathing—"in through the nose, out through the mouth"; in through the mouth and out through the nose seemed to be his method—nor had he been instructed in yoga exercises for the rest of his body, yet these were two things that would have helped him so much. Yoga breathing and yoga exercise for the whole world! you had to think when you saw this man. And a macrobiotic diet, too.

There was no way the man's pants could stay up around his beachball-size abdominal area—an area only partially concealed beneath his shirt, which was always missing a button or two and even had a shirttail hanging out sometimes. The last time I had seen an abdominal area of this type was on the world-renowned reproductive surgeon Dr. Arnold Loquesto, whom I'd consulted and photographed, and I'd never gotten over the sight. I'd seen it on one of my trips to photograph the surgeon when he wasn't in the mood to have his picture taken. He was sitting on a couch and trying out his new blue-and-white-striped bathing trunks as he read his mail, even though it was winter. His eleven-year-old son had called me into the room to prove a fact he had looked up in a book. He stood at his father's side waving his hand like a circus barker toward the fact in the book. The surgeon and his abdominal area seemed to be bathed in a golden light, as if they'd been painted by a Flemish master, but this effect might have been caused by my attempt to avert my eyes from the sight too quickly.

But at Discount Drugs there were only fluorescent lights and not the recessed ceiling lights the surgeon's architect had chosen. In this light I saw that the manager wore navy blue slacks with faded navy blue areas. With those trousers he wore a grayish-white shirt—"what we're ordered to wear by headquarters." The shirt could never be whitened, no matter how many gallons of Clorox were used to wash it, because it was 100 percent polyester.

I knew this man from all the times I'd asked him to lead me to the Dentemp I needed to glue in a temporary crown. A dentist and his lab had made a crown the wrong color so many times that I had an ill-fitting temporary one falling out for two years. The manager liked to say "Dentie-temp, aisle four." I loved to hear him say it, because it sounded like a nickname for the product.

This year, before I knew it, the Valentine display had been replaced with a new, expanded Easter display of frightening pastel colors. I was disappointed to see a five-foot stack of cardboard boxes filled with red hearts being returned to the warehouse. Either they'd be back next year, or they'd be expired and sent to the Iraqis or the Russians. "We get all expired foodstuffs," I'd heard the Kurds and Russians complaining on CNN. Right after Valentine's Day, I bought up all the boxes of chocolate turtles for my Swedish friend to take with her on her trip to Sweden. I hoped to prove that there was one good kind of ordinary American candy, after she told me about the delicious, healthful candy they had in Sweden. "In Sweden the candy is *good*!" she said. "In Sweden the candy is not sweet!" But when I checked the turtle box I discovered that the turtles were from Canada.

The one candy I knew of that tasted good and was good for you was Japanese macrobiotic rice-syrup taffy. It was also good for removing temporary crowns when the dentist couldn't do it. "I'll have to tap it out," the dentist had said. Then he took a small dental sledgehammer and hammered at the crown for several minutes before he gave up and I mentioned the taffy. He admitted that another patient had to use Jujubes for the same purpose. This dentist wasn't intelligent but had mastered the technique of saying "How are you doing?" while he was sledgehammering the crown or drilling the remaining tooth down to a stump without using Novocain. I knew that this was the kind of thing dentists and doctors were taught to say. I figured it out when, on one of my trips to photograph Dr. Loquesto, the surgeon was speeding down a truck-filled highway and I was one of his passengers. I asked him to go slower and he yelled, "No! Why should I go slower?"

"We're in the right lane and we're passing that big truck," I said.

"Look, we're past already," he said, and then I remembered that this was the same technique he used for medical procedures. If the patient complained he'd say, "It's over already. How can it hurt?" Or his own special trick—"I haven't done anything yet. How can it hurt?"

My feeling of luckiness increased when I saw I had two places to spend the holidays this year. Discount Drugs was renovated; headquarters decided to widen the aisles, repair the leak-stained ceilings, and install a pharmacy. I looked forward to the arrival of the prescription department—even though I use herbal tinctures from health-food stores—because I like to watch pharmacists talking while staring down and counting pills. The "hygienic pill-counting tray" is a favorite of mine. The store would have the new ceiling, too—as important to me as the restoration of the ceiling of the Sistine Chapel was to others—and now I would have two pharmacists to watch and maybe even to talk to. It turned out that one of the pharmacists knew Dr. Loquesto from his last drugstore job in Massachusetts. He said he'd worked with the surgeon's hospital, and then told me his own plans for which hospitals he'd go to for various emergencies. "An accident—a limb is severed—I'm packed in ice and flown to New York" was one scheme.

I had to hope Easter would be over early this year when I saw the new expanded Easter display of woven-plastic grass and chocolate rabbits—all topped off with big stuffed toy rabbits and wrapped in yellow cellophane. I began to wonder where did Jesus fit in with Easter decorations. Where was Jesus was something I'd been wondering on and off since last year, when I'd heard a middle-of-the-night TV program starting with the question: "What is the consciousness of a frog?" and leading up to the idea that Jesus was everywhere.

They tried to make the program sound scientific—they started out with a bunch of professors and scientists telling about a frog's mind and a human brain—but all this was beating around the bush and leading up to God and Jesus. It had that God-and-Jesus creeping edge the whole time, and was followed by an even sneakier show proclaiming that there was an answer to problems between husbands and wives. The show was hosted by Dick Clark, who had a new, tragic look that he tried to perk up with interested smiles from time to time. All those watching would have to feel bad and old when they remembered seeing him as the host of "American Bandstand" compared with his descent to acting as a shill for a mass-marriage counselor. After about an hour of the counselor's hinting at "all the things you men do to hurt your wives each and every day," the main thing turned out to be not talking. Next he said that women spoke a few hundred thousand words a day and men spoke only around sixty thousand. When men came home at night, they had used up their quota. That was why they had nothing to say.

My husband liked to say, "You knew when you married me that I didn't talk." What I didn't know was that Tourette's syndrome was his favorite disease to read about, because it was a disease he wished he had. It was an exaggeration of his own personality—yell a few words, sometimes obscene, make faces, try to act things out rather than speak a word or two.

At the end of the sales pitch for the video on communication and saved marriages, the counselor, with Dick Clark's help, finally gave the biggest pitch of all. He'd been saving it up for the grand finale. It was something like "And do you ladies want to know the one thing you do that makes your husbands feel as bad as they make you feel?" The ladies did want to know and I wanted to know, too, just as I wanted to know about the consciousness of a frog and the whereabouts of Jesus. But you had to send for the tape to find out.

The whereabouts of Jesus was on my mind as usual when I saw the Schoenfeld brothers walking along a tree-shaded street on a warm, humid evening last November in East Hampton. It was the time of gloom that came after the Supreme Court confirmation hearings.

I had first seen these brothers at the bottom of the cliff at Cliff Beach in Nantucket fifteen years earlier. The brothers were walking along together near the water. I had biked to the beach to watch the sun set, and no one was around except some people on their porch up on the cliff. These people were drinking their way through the sunset hour. The brothers were very white. They appeared to be in their early fifties. As they climbed the long wooden stairway to the top of the cliff, I saw that they had wavy light-red hair, and when they got to the top step and said hello I saw that they had light-green eyes. Since they were at least a generation older than I was, it seemed safe to talk to them. They weren't tall and they were thin, but not like the man in the ad "I used to be a ninety-eight-pound weakling." They had the amount of muscle development that people used to have from doing normal athletic activities rather than going to gyms. They wore navy-blue bathing trunks, and each one carried a worn-out white towel with faded stripes. After we exchanged pleasantries—and everything anyone said to me in Nantucket seemed to be a pleasantry, because I still lived in New York, where life was a hell—the brothers put on their sandals and left Cliff Beach.

I immediately began to wonder about them. They looked as if they were used to spending their time in each other's company. What had gone wrong in their childhood was something I wondered, even though I was not a psychiatrist. The last time I had wondered what was wrong with someone, a certain endodontist who behaved like an inmate of an insane asylum, the woman I was discussing him with—a cashier at a health-food store—said, "Why are you a psychiatrist?"

Among the pleasantries I'd exchanged with the Schoenfeld brothers that day was a discussion of where the good swimming was. "How can you swim amongst the waves?" one of the brothers asked. He was the more talkative of the two. The other, less interested brother hovered behind him.

Every summer after that I'd see the brothers at Cliff Beach. After a few years they told me their names, and sometimes my husband and I would spot them at night walking around the town. I never saw them with anyone but each other.

A few years after our first meeting, on an afternoon in September when the light was too good to enter the East Hampton A&P to buy a lemon, I went into an overpriced small store that the permanent residents never patronized. I thought that this one time it would be O.K. to pay forty cents for a lemon. I recognized a man who was looking at jars of mustard. He was looking at them without any real purpose. I couldn't remember how I knew him, but then I realized that he was one of the Schoenfeld brothers, the less talkative one. I figured that the talkative brother was in a different aisle. After we said hello I decided to say, "I thought I recognized you from Nantucket."

"Oh, yes—that's it," he said, as if he didn't care one way or the other. "What are you doing here?"

"We live here, but we go away for the summer."

"We do the same thing. It's far superior there. The swimming is better. You don't have the crowds, the bad element." By the bad element he meant a woman I had just seen enter the store. She was dressed like Chiquita Banana, but she wasn't wearing any bananas. She was wearing golden, banana-colored toreador pants, tight and shiny; her midsection was bare, and she wore banana-gold wedgies and large disk-shaped earrings almost the same size as disks for a CD player. She wore a white turban and lots of bracelets, and a gold belt made up of many gold disks. She had red nail polish on her long fingernails and her toenails.

"I guess we'd never see anyone like that in Nantucket," I said.

"No," the brother said, shrinking away from the sight.

After this incident I saw the brothers all around East Hampton and even once in Southampton, at a vegetarian restaurant. The brothers didn't seem to mind the sloppiness and hippieness of the place and were eating sprout sandwiches. There was a rumor that anytime people ate at this place they got sick. The brothers said they had just discovered this restaurant and wasn't it good? What could I say? I said yes. Probably the sprouts had been grown in a dank basement under the store.

The brothers said they'd be off to Nantucket soon. They asked me where our house was and I told them in a way no one could understand. I didn't think I'd want to find anyone else walking down that lane, a lane traversed by only five or seven people a day. Once, when I was standing outside staring at the garden, a man biking down the lane stopped to ask me the question "Is this your house?" I had to say no—we rented it every year. I wanted to say yes, we owned it, but Nantucket was too small to get away with a lie about that house, because it was the most desired house on the island. Although it had only one bedroom, it had four fireplaces and four bathrooms and was on the most beautiful lane in Nantucket, if not in the whole world. Sometimes when I came out in the morning I'd find a painter painting a picture of the house. Once a German tourist dared to ask me how he might rent the house. "You may never rent it," I wanted to say, but I restricted myself to saying that the owners lived there all the other months—a lie. Many people, including me, wanted to buy this house, even though my husband said he hated it because there wasn't one comfortable place to sit. When I repeated this to a neighbor, she said, "Yes, well, men are strange."

The man on the bike didn't look like a Nantucketer, he looked like a New Yorker; he had a hunched-over, beaten-down New York–intellectual look. Just so he wouldn't feel too bad I told him about a slew of terrible houses we'd rented from dishonest real-estate agents before we'd found this house by accident. As soon as I said "dishonest" the man guessed the names of the agents, and began to tell about the houses they'd rented him, the intentional misrepresentations of the houses, the lies he'd been told, the things that were wrong with the houses, the ulcers they'd exacerbated, and how he didn't have the strength to fight these agents because of his ulcers and his work—a philosophical, historical discourse on an era I'd never heard of. His house this time, he complained, was drab and ugly, and had no "objets d'art." I said that our house had none of those, either, and that we had to bring a carton of our own things every year to make it light and summery. Then the beaten-down intellectual asked if he could have a look inside the house. I said that my husband was taking a nap, and the house was so tiny that there was no way to enter without waking him. This was the truth. The man seemed disappointed and looked longingly toward the windows he was hoping to peer through to see some objets d'art. I swear there are no objets d'art, I wanted to tell him, but instead made up the lie that the whole house was painted dull gray. And also how I had to run from room to room to cover all the dark furniture with white cotton sheets the minute we arrived. He seemed to feel better as I went on—it was all so realistic, he could tell from his years of house-renting that it had to be true. He finally lost interest and went on his way. I could see him planning his return to his wretched garret to get back to work on his intellectual œuvre.

Maybe if I simply said "Yes" or "No" or "Good evening," the way other people did, I could have spent my time more profitably. I didn't yet know the busy surgeon Dr. Loquesto, so I hadn't learned from his example to "keep moving."

One September evening in Nantucket—it was a few months after I'd met the brothers eating sprouts in Southampton—I was biking back from Cliff Beach past the Congregational church, and I saw a group of people going up the steps to the beautiful white building. I looked at the billboard to see if there was a film festival—maybe *The Stranger* would be playing. But it wasn't a film festival, it was a Jewish High Holy Day service being held at the church. This was something I wanted to check out.

I wasn't much more inappropriately dressed than the other people I saw going in. I was wearing a long, faded blue cotton skirt and a faded pink T-shirt, but the T-shirt was from France and had small shoulder pads. I had some thin white ankle socks under my nonleather walking sandals and these two things—the shoulder pads and the thin socks—made me think I could go up to the doorway and peek inside. One thing I wanted to see was what had been done with the Cross.

About a hundred people had turned out for the service. They were people I'd seen all my life in Nantucket. Some looked happy and some looked nervous, and I wondered whether this was really such a good idea, to take over the Congregational church. Even though they hadn't taken it over by force, the way students took over college buildings in the sixties. Probably they were just happy that they didn't have to go back to Boston or some other hot city and could stay in this paradise without feeling that it was a sin. A few older women wore real dresses, but they were plain cotton dresses. No one wore jewelry or even pearls. Some of the men wore sports jackets but only two wore ties.

I was standing in the back watching the service proceed. Even though it was in English I couldn't follow it. Then I saw two other people standing and watching from the side of the room. These two were the Schoenfeld brothers. They were wearing khaki Bermuda shorts and white Lacoste shirts with alligators on the chest. Then I saw the Cross. It was covered up with a piece of dark-blue fabric. In front of the covered Cross was an ark with Hebrew scrolls underneath blue velvet. I wondered whose job the covering of the Cross had been— was it the job of a Congregationalist or a Jew, and which case would have been worse if viewed by Patrick Buchanan. I couldn't think of a scenario that would reflect well on either religion, even though the Congregationalists must have offered the church and probably even suggested ways to hide the Cross.

After watching the Schoenfelds and taking a count of all the shorts and polo shirts in the room, I began to feel bored. The doors were open and two large standing fans were going, but outside the doors I saw trees and leaves and sky. I thought it would be better to be out under those trees than inside the complicated atmosphere of the Congregational church.

Once out in the air, I wondered why I kept meeting the brothers everywhere.

One evening the next year, I was in Nantucket and my husband was called away—his clients were in a hurry to make plans for their unsightly buildings. I met the brothers on Main Street and found out some more information. They were court stenographers. They lived in Southampton all year in different apartments in the same neighborhood. They left Southampton only to go to East Hampton and Nantucket. They came to Nantucket for the summer and stayed in a hotel. I listened to each brother telling what his hotel room was like, and this was confusing, because sometimes I couldn't be sure which brother was which. If my husband had been around he wouldn't have wanted to talk with the brothers at such length. He referred to my acquaintances with people as aimless, futile encounters. He preferred dogs to people, and he wanted to have as few human encounters as possible.

It was a night in Nantucket one recent summer when I understood that lots of men had this problem. I had just seen one of the brothers walking alone, and I was afraid that something had happened to the other one. I parked my bicycle near a bench on the sidewalk and went up the steps to an antiques store that had some ship paintings in the window. All the ones I liked were eight hundred or two thousand dollars, but I saw a crude-looking one for only four hundred. Parts of the boat weren't painted but glued and pasted on. The clouds were made of cotton balls, and the sails were tied on with string, which was knotted on the back of the canvas. The saleswoman said she liked it, and didn't it look like something a family had worked on together? I had no personal knowledge of any such wholesome family activities, but I went along with it and said yes. "This looks like the kind of thing my four sons might have done with their dad as a family project," she said. I suddenly became alarmed by the woman's wholesomeness—she wasn't old enough to have been a parent in the nineteen-fifties, the great era of American family life, she was only about fifty-eight. But maybe she was from Minnesota or someplace where these activities still went on. Then I said that my husband would come see the painting when he came back up. "It would be good for his study, wouldn't it?" she said. I felt I could tell her that our house was so small he didn't have a study and that our variance to build one had been denied. I explained what a blow this was, since I had hoped to move the television into the study so I would never again have to hear that switching around with the remote control.

The woman assumed we owned a house in Nantucket. "You know, one of the builders is building these little dog-houses," she said. "They're really cute, too—they were meant for dogs originally, but people are using them for other purposes. A man and his TV is a very popular use, I hear."

"I don't think we have enough land even for that," I said.

"It's only about eight by ten," she said. "That would give him room for his chair and his TV," she said. "And a small table for a glass and a beer bottle."

Although I hadn't described my husband, his chair, his TV, and his glass in his hand—his best friend was this glass—the wholesome woman had the exact picture. I looked into her eyes, and she looked into my eyes, and we both smiled. Then I laughed, and she kept smiling. It was her acceptance of what husbands do. It was the idea of her four sons working with their dad on family art projects even though she was probably in the kitchen at the time frying up bacon in a skillet and cooking all kinds of other animal fats—fried eggs, sausages, Spam, and even that meat with cheese and olives smashed into it, or is it cheese with meat and olives smashed in? Her past seemed too wholesome and American, even though since I was a child I'd been trying to pick up a sense of family life from people like this in places like Nantucket. I looked at the woman's smile, her face, her chin-length pin-curled white hair, and her slightly buck teeth, and I realized that she looked exactly like Dwight D. Eisenhower. It wasn't what she was talking about, either—she really looked like him.

I was falling into a trance that enabled me to imagine the people speaking turning into what they were speaking about.

Maybe this was some kind of psychological disorder on my part. As I looked into the eyes of the speakers, something turned them into the substance of their subject matter. This happened most often when I watched "Crossfire" on CNN. I watched this show mainly for entertainment. Also I thought I could get some pointers on how to tell lies in a smooth way. It was during an argument by Patrick Buchanan that I felt a transformation taking place. He was yelling things about the "viable fetus," and I wondered when it was that every common person learned when a fetus was what. Facts about fetuses were now known by just about everyone on TV.

During this angry shouting of the word "fetus" by Patrick Buchanan, I saw that he knew deep in his heart and brain and soul what a fetus was. Whenever I pictured the tiny fetus at its early stages of development I always had sympathy for it and hoped it wouldn't be aborted. But Patrick Buchanan himself had been a fetus, I understood as he said the word over and over, and then I began to picture him as a fetus. He was one of the ones that survived. I tried to picture the more intelligent and admirable commentators as fetuses, but when their turns came up for the final rebuttal, none seemed to be that admirable or intelligent. Only Michael Kinsley had the right to life.

I left the antiques store without any sailboat painting for my husband's study or doghouse. Then I saw the brother again. He was slithering down the outside of the street and there was no way to avoid a meeting. It was the background brother this time. He said that they'd had dinner in town and that he was on his way back to his hotel. Then he asked about which restaurants we went to. As I told him where we went, I began to wonder why we kept going to Nantucket every summer. Our life there sounded so dull. And as I realized now how dull these evenings sounded, I remembered that Dr. Loquesto had warned me of this. "What do you want to go there for? You just go to the beach. How dull!" When I said we didn't stay at the beach but biked into the sunset and walked through the moors picking beach plums, he yelled, "Even worse!" And when I gave his family some beach-plum jelly I'd made from the picked plums, he tasted it and made a face.

The brother and I walked down Main Street toward Orange Street. We agreed that there was really no other place we'd rather be than Nantucket. As we neared his hotel I told him that we lived right nearby and asked if he would like to see our house. He said all right, in a nervous way. As we went down the dark lane that led to our moonlit white garden he said, "I didn't know there were any little houses back here."

Unlike the downtrodden intellectual who wanted to see our house so badly, the Schoenfeld brother didn't seem eager for the house tour I was planning for him. I felt as if I were dragging him down the lane along with my heavy, old Raleigh bike.

"We've walked by this field of wildflowers and this veg-etable farm, but I don't remember any little house," he said with anxiety.

Perhaps the brother thought that I had a romantic interest in him. If I had a romantic interest in any man, I'd never invite him to see a lane or a house. I would have to ignore the man completely. Didn't the brother know how these things worked? Instead of being astounded by the beauty of the lane and the tiny house, he became more jittery as he said, "I never knew a house was here."

We went into the house through the kitchen, which held no interest for him. Then I led him into the dining room, which was filled with my work and my husband's work—papers, photographs, boxes, and books. Next I took him through the first sitting room into the second sitting room, where I suggested that he sit down. I pointed out three of the fireplaces, but even this didn't interest him.

"Well, yes, this is perfect," he said. "What more could you want?"

"Bigger rooms. More rooms," I said.

"How expensive is a place like this?" he asked.

I made up a price I thought sounded reasonable. The whole town doesn't have to know the rent.

"That's reasonable," he said.

"You and your brother could rent a little house, too."

"It wouldn't be feasible. We like to dine out."

"You wouldn't have to stay home just because you had a kitchen."

"Well, there are other reasons. For you it's different. You're a married couple. We need a different kind of situation—the opportunity to meet people."

"Meet people?" I said. I thought of all the people I'd met just going out of the door of this house.

"There's more chance for other kinds of things."

"Other things?" I said.

"Well . . . female companionship," he said.

"Oh," I said. I was surprised to hear this phrase. While I was trying to pull myself together and recover from hearing the words, I tried to formulate a sentence about the ease of meeting people on a small island—a sentence like that. Then

I tried to change the subject but I knew that we were out of subjects. We had talked about every subject we'd ever be able to talk about.

The next and last time I saw the brothers was in East Hampton. It was that warm November evening. My husband and I were riding our bicycles near the town pond when I thought I saw the two men looking at some flowers in front of an inn next to the pond.

"Aren't those your friends?" my husband asked.

I didn't want to know what they were up to. They seemed to be scouting out the premises, checking the landscaping and the porch, and sizing up the inn. But they had a furtive way of doing the scouting, instead of walking right up the path and in the door.

"They're not my friends," I told my husband.

He shook his head with disapproval as we continued our ride into the murky evening.

When we got back to the pond it was almost dusk, but I could still see well enough to spot the brothers coming toward us from the direction of the beach.

"We have to say hello to your friends this time," my husband said.

After saying hello, the more talkative one asked where we were going. I said that we weren't going anywhere, we were on our way home.

"You live around here?" the brother asked, looking at the big old houses everywhere.

"We live in the one small house in the neighborhood," I said. It was true.

I didn't expect anything about current events to come up, so the next question was a surprise. "What did you think of the confirmation hearings?" the talkative brother asked.

"Sickening," I said. I really began to feel sick.

"Wasn't it a disgusting spectacle?" he asked, looking at my husband.

"Don't ask him," I said. "He's on his way to the conservative side."

Both brothers looked at my husband with disbelief and little weird smiles.

"There was one conservative Democratic senator from Connecticut who voted no," I said.

"He's an Orthodox Jew, too," the brother said.

"Is there a connection?" I asked.

"Maybe it gives him some moral decency," he said.

"What about Christians?" I said. "Jesus would have voted no."

"What do you think of our senators?" the other brother asked. "Aren't they deplorable?"

"We have to get rid of them," I said. "And the President, too."

"We must organize and defeat them," he said with feverish energy.

Then another surprise question.

"Will you be here Thanksgiving? Do you come here for Christmas?" the talkative one asked. For a second I thought they knew of an upcoming political event to help defeat the senators and President.

"Yes," I said. I decided right then that if I was ever going to be there for Thanksgiving, the brothers would be invited to a Thanksgiving vegetarian dinner. As I was trying to drum up a guest list from the few people we knew, most of whom, including us, had to go to grim family dinners, the brother said, "What about Christmas, what about Christmas?"

"We're always here," I said. "Aren't you?"

"No, we like to go someplace different. This year I thought I'd like to go somewhere in the Berkshires. To an inn up in Massachusetts or somewhere."

"That's a good idea," I said. "We did that once, before we lived here."

"You did? You went to the Berkshires? Was it nice?"

"Yes," I said. "We were trying to decide whether to move up there."

"It was beautiful," my husband said without feeling. He described a snowy winter scene in a standard way.

"Did you stay in an inn? Do you know any inns up there?" the brother asked.

"Yes," I said. "We stayed in Stockbridge. At a famous old inn. It was right before Christmas."

"Was it nice? Was the food good? Did they have a Christmas tree?"

"Yes, really nice. They had a vegetable plate on the menu. It even had brown rice on it. They had a tree—a big tree."

"Was the food good?" the less interested, more subdued brother asked.

"You know what her idea of good is," my husband said.

"What kind of food do they serve?" the subdued brother asked.

"Normal American food," my husband said. "But healthier, because of the hippie influx of the seventies."

"And the Stockbridge School and the sanitarium," I said.

"Are there Christmas decorations? Do they have a nice tree?" the brother asked.

"Yes, beautiful decorations. A big tree," I said. I was getting worried.

"Is it in Lenox? Do you know any place in Lenox?"

"It's in Stockbridge. But there is one in Lenox. You can look in an inn book."

"What kind of people go there? Are there people you could have an intelligent conversation with? Are there congenial people?"

"There were intelligent-looking people when we were there in 1977." I remembered the people and realized that they were all talking to each other in the groups they'd gone to the inn with. A family dinner of eight. A group of six professors and doctors in tweed clothing. Grandmothers with white hair, people smiling at their families, out for pre-Christmas celebrations. I wondered what the chances were of any of these groups meeting up with the brothers. Were they looking for people to discuss the confirmation hearings with? The topic would be finished by December, I thought.

The last time we'd stayed at an inn—a few weeks before—was at the height of that topic's popularity. We'd had to watch those hearings in the library of an inn in Maine, a library filled with old Republicans. The inn was so backward that a vegetable plate was served with sausages mixed into stewed tomatoes. We watched the hearings while waiting for the right day to meet Dr. Loquesto in his laboratory for a new reproductive technique. In the laboratory the doctor became enraged when a machine didn't work, and he slammed out of the room before I could ask him to hand me the *Times*. But maybe it was all for the best not to be reading that testimony while conception might be taking place. Instead, I could wonder how the surgeon had come to act like the crazed professor in *The Blue Angel.*

"He's afraid the roads will be icy," the talkative brother said.

"But it never snows anymore," I said.

"Is there a train?" he asked. "Did you drive?"

"We drove," my husband said, "but the roads were clear. They're main roads."

"I don't like to drive in snow," the quieter brother said.

"It never snows," I said. "But whenever you're there it's already snowed a few days before."

"We wanted to see snow. Here it never snows," the talkative brother said.

"It snowed three feet two years ago," I said.

"Do you know any inns in Lenox?" he asked.

"We went there only one time and we stayed in Stockbridge," my husband said. "It was the only place we knew about." He was ready to pedal off, I could tell.

"What were the rooms like?"

"They were good. Some were a little run-down. But it's all redone now," I said.

"Did they have Christmas decorations?"

"You mean you want to go to a place where it's really like Christmas?" I said.

"That's why we want to go. Here it's dreary, it's not like Christmas."

"Norman Rockwell lived there," I said.

"Were the decorations nice? The Christmas decorations? The tree?"

"Yes, yes, all those things. A big tree with ornaments," I said.

"What was it like? Were the ornaments lovely?"

"Yes, yes. I didn't want to leave. I wanted to live there," I said.

"At the inn?" the more anxious brother asked.

"Yes, at the inn or in a house up there. Anything."

"Was it in Lenox?"

"No," I said, "Stockbridge." I didn't know what else to say.

"We better be going," my husband said. "Have a good trip."

"Yes," I said. "Go to the Berkshires. Look in an inn book."

"O.K.," the brother said.

The brother in the background sent a weak smile in my direction. They weren't dressed for the greenhouse weather. I'd been noticing this the whole time. They thought that because it was November they should wear crewneck sweaters over their shirts, but they were wrong. The frantic brother was perspiring during most of the conversation. The other brother had looked on with tolerance of his odd sibling.

As we rode away, I said to my husband, "Well, what did you think of that?"

"Those are some brothers," he said.

"What was their childhood like? How did it happen?"

My husband shook his head. "I was afraid they wanted to come see our house," he said. "And I wanted to watch the end of the game."

"No, they just want to do something for Christmas. They're just trying to celebrate the Christmas season."

"I guess so."

"I hope they go away and have a good time."

"I hope so, too."

"Maybe we should have a dinner and invite them."

"Who else could we invite?"

"I can't think of anyone." I wished I could think of the right people. Some relatives of Bishop Fulton Sheen lived around the corner. We had our Swedish friends, but they'd be busy with some meatball festival. Maybe the manager of Discount Drugs would be free.

I thought about the brothers trying to celebrate the Christmas season in the Berkshires, in Stockbridge or Lenox. It was so much fun when we were there the last time, when we were a newly married young couple. I remembered the old Viennese psychiatrist saying to Ingrid Bergman in the Alfred Hitchcock film *Spellbound,* "There's nothing so nice as a new marriage—no psychoses yet, no aggressions, no guilt complexes." I remembered the dining room and the families and the vegetable plate on the menu and the snow-covered hills and beautiful old houses and the cleared roads. The lock on our car door had frozen and my husband had to unfreeze it by lighting matches, one after another until he'd used up a whole matchbook with the inn's name printed on it. I remembered the Christmas tree and the faded English china on the mantelpiece. I pictured the whole room, with the fireplace and the pine needles and the light blue china everywhere. Just the way a real American home is supposed to be at Christmas. I pictured the families and the big Christmas tree with the lovely ornaments.

"Maybe we should go up there for Christmas this year, too," I said.

"Where?" my husband asked. "Stockbridge?"

"Or Lenox. Anywhere. We went once. Remember? We had a good time."

THE THRILL IS GONE

I had a headache. I was in my favorite place—Nantucket, Massachusetts—but my head ached anyway. I was glad to have the headache, because I'd read in a manual of natural remedies that a cure for a headache was one or two cups of black coffee. It would work only for those who didn't consume caffeine on a regular basis, or on any basis. Having given up coffee fifteen years before, I tried the remedy this year and found that it worked. Not only did it work, but I rediscovered the fun of caffeine and often found myself wondering hopefully if any little twinge was a headache coming on.

On this day, I lay in bed for a while trying to decide whether to drink black coffee or to take three Tylenol tablets. It wasn't good to wake up with a headache, but I'd read in a different manual that certain headaches were caused by progesterone occurring normally in the cycles of women of child-bearing age. It was either the progesterone surge or the sudden drop-off, I couldn't remember which. I had asked the world-renowned reproductive surgeon Dr. Arnold Loquesto, whom I'd consulted and photographed, and he said, "Ask Stevens. He published a whole paper about it."

"But what does it say is the cause?"

"How should I know? I don't even believe in it!" he yelled. Then he ran off to an operating room, or a conference in Australia.

As I lay in bed with the pounding on the side of my head, I looked out at the garden of our rented house, a garden still in full bloom, even though it was August—the month that was often given as a reason gardens were out of bloom—and with self-loathing I remembered the character Oblomov. I compared my lying in bed and looking at the garden, the quince tree, the bumblebees, white butterflies, and chirping birds while trying to decide between a caffeine fix and a pharmaceutical one—with the lying in bed of Oblomov. I felt myself to be a wastrel and my life to have been wasted. My adult life, anyway. In my childhood, I might have worked harder and been more worthwhile. Certainly, I looked better and was cuter. I tried to think of my contribution to society, family, or community. I compared myself with Hillary Clinton. Even though she was not as admired as Jacqueline Kennedy—I always compared myself unfavorably with her, too—I saw that Hillary had worked harder in college than I had. Then she worked hard in law school, and as a litigation partner at her law firm, and at looking so well groomed and alert ever since that bus tour through the hot countryside. I bet she had some coffee every day.

Sometimes I compared myself with Princess Diana, and even there I didn't do well. Actually, I had the most in common with her, being a vegetarian, but—the lucky Princess—her husband was one, too, whereas mine liked to order little

ducks and livers and eat them in front of me. That, and a fear
of gaining weight—I'd read in *Star* that servants had found
the Princess in the kitchen one night wolfing down an entire
meat pie. I knew that this couldn't be true, since she would
have been wolfing down some other kind of pie, under the
compulsion to do some midnight eating.

With these thoughts never far from my mind—these, plus
comparisons with women, couples, and happy families I saw
on television commercials—I found it hard to get out of bed.
Bed—what could be a more pleasant place to be? I got up. I
opened the French doors to the garden and breathed the air,
and I realized that outside would be a better place to be—
right in the perennial border, deadheading lavender and rose
blossoms, with the bees buzzing and the butterflies floating
and the birds chirping all around me.

But before I could get out into that garden I had to get rid
of the headache. I looked at my bottle of Tylenol and then
thought of the cups of black coffee. Both seemed wrong. I had
taken too much Tylenol in my life, for dental procedures and
female complaints. It didn't work for either but was a necessary first step on the road to the hard stuff of codeine and
ibuprofen. I pictured my liver—what it might look like from
processing the number of medications it had been served up—
and then I pictured my circulatory system, my blood vessels
dilating and contracting from the caffeine they'd been forced
to take in. Immediately, I saw that my liver looked worse.
I chose the caffeine.

But I found that I didn't have any left because my last two
headaches had used up the organically grown coffee beans I
kept in the freezer for medicinal purposes. Most people don't
know that coffee beans are one of the most heavily sprayed

crops, just as the makers of Pepperidge Farm cookies and Cape Cod Potato Chips don't know that cottonseed oil has the most pesticide residue of any cooking oil, since the cotton bolls aren't subject to food-crop rules and are sprayed heavily for the cotton crop. And I'd had such happy memories of the boll weevil since being forced to sing in sixth-grade assembly a song called "De Boll Weevil," after reciting the Lord's Prayer.

I took a shower and dressed myself just to the point of decency for being seen buying coffee beans. I wondered whether I should put on some mascara, recently having heard Coco Chanel say in a filmed interview that women had to dress well, even when going to the grocery store, because they owed it to society, and also because any day, any time, might be their date with destiny—the moment they could meet that special man. The special-man part—screw that. But owing it to society made sense. My cruelty-free cosmetics were in the upstairs bathroom. The downstairs bathrooms had been designed by an architect who specialized in designing prisons and they were too small to keep any cosmetics in and too dark to see to put them on. I forced myself to go up the steep staircase at the other end of the house to the sweltering upstairs bathroom. It had no insulation and was too hot to stay in even to put on a small amount of makeup. I wet my face and quickly put on some Vegelatum—a nonpetroleum jelly. I'd read in a fashion magazine a list of commandments which included "Never wash your face without moisturizing immediately." If only there were a way to put on a little makeup without having to see your face, I was thinking as I tried to gear up for the task.

My eyelids were still puffy, even though I'd given up taking Xanax for insomnia and switched over to valerian-root tincture. Maybe it was because I took twice the recommended dose after reading "ten to twenty drops, or as needed." This must have been what Marilyn Monroe's and Elvis Presley's lives were like: "Downers to sleep and uppers to wake," I'd read. At least I had never smoked marijuana, and this was always on my mind because of the presidential campaign.

I was planning to wear sunglasses with darker clip-ons on top of them, so why did I need the mascara, I asked myself. In case someone could see through the lenses when I removed the clip-ons in order to pay for the coffee beans. That special someone. The two specials I had ever hoped to meet—Elvis Presley and President Kennedy—were both dead, although I saw headlines about their being alive whenever I passed the magazine rack in the supermarket. It was more likely that I'd see Ted Kennedy, since sightings of him were reported at the farm where we bought corn and tomatoes every day. One afternoon, I'd heard the farmer tell his wife that he'd seen Ted, barefoot, at the pizzeria the night before.

So if Ted Kennedy was barefoot, overweight, and sun-damaged, not to mention the condition of his liver, why did I need to dress decently and put on mascara to buy coffee beans? Because of the failure of the feminist movement, I figured as I separated my lashes with a tiny steel comb. In fact, I wasn't dressed decently, since the hem on my skirt was coming down and I hadn't bothered even to pin it up. The week before, I'd put a paper clip on the hem to keep it up, but on this hot morning I didn't have the energy to look for a paper clip. I didn't have the mental energy to do anything anymore—I had to force myself to do my once favorite things, like going to Nantucket at all that summer. The thrill was gone.

I tried to remember which poem the line "My heart leaps up" came from. Instead I thought of my second-grade teacher, Miss Wagstaff, an overweight, elderly spinster with dyed red hair cut in a Buster Brown style, and a face like his dog, Tige, but powdered white, with pink rouge in the wrong places. She'd worn a gray jacket every day of the school week, and the elbows of the jacket were frayed away to nothing. One day, during rest period, when we were supposed to be resting or reading, I noticed her taking off her jacket. She went to a closet and took out a box. Then she spread the jacket across her desk and opened the box. She took out a pair of scissors and a spool of thread. We began to whisper to each other, "Miss Wagstaff is sewing her jacket!" But then, to our amazement, she took out a roll of Scotch tape and began to tape the worn part of the sleeve. (And this was the era before matte-finish tape was invented, too.) One piece this way, another that way—maybe four or five pieces until the job was done. When I told my parents what had happened, they didn't believe the story, and even though Miss Wagstaff wasn't a fit teacher in any other way, they allowed me to remain in that public school. I thought that my public-school background was one reason Hillary Clinton and Jacqueline Kennedy and Princess Diana had achieved more than I had and were better groomed than I was.

On the other hand, my loss of enthusiasm for everything could have been due to other factors. I'd recently heard David Letterman ask B. B. King to sing "The Thrill Is Gone." Dave said that he personally understood what it meant. Perhaps the feeling had nothing to do with a public-school background but with that other thing—the over-forty sense of various problems and disappointments people feel before getting into the next phase of life, where they're simply glad to be alive, having accepted the loss of youth and the hope that any of their dreams for the world might come true. "Just look around at your own community—the overdevelopment of cities and land in the last ten years," I'd heard someone say in an environmental minute on television. Was it Robert Redford or Paul Newman speaking? I couldn't remember, but whoever it was, he didn't tell anything you could do about it. Maybe it was Paul Newman, since I remembered my husband giving the excuse for buying Paul Newman's popcorn kernels, instead of Orville Redenbacher's. "He gives away the money to charities you like."

I opened the front door. Outside, it was that time of hot, empty stillness I dreaded each day. No one was around. All the normal, healthy people of this Nantucket neighborhood had done their early-morning errands and were off doing something worthwhile and probably aerobic. This hot, lonely time lasted from noon to five each day. I would be the only one in the neighborhood stumbling out a rose-covered doorway into high noon, and it reminded me of high noon in that movie whenever I had to face a showdown with the sun.

I'd left the car windows open all night so that it wouldn't be too hot inside. I turned the air conditioner on and pulled out of the crushed-seashell driveway. But I kept the windows open, and I recalled the outrage Dr. Loquesto had expressed for driving with air-conditioning on and windows open. He said his mother used the same system in her house, and it made him really mad when he saw it. But on the one occasion I went to photograph her for my series of photographs of mothers of reproductive surgeons, I found that she had the heat on and the windows closed when the temperature outside was seventy-five degrees.

Anything could happen on the road to the coffee store. And whatever happened to me would be what I deserved for driving to a place I should have biked to before the sun was so high and so hot. But I put my seat belt on anyway, still having the will to live and also to avoid encounters with plastic surgeons in the Nantucket Cottage Hospital emergency room. I'd once seen a general surgeon in the Finast parking lot. He looked more like an eagle than a human except for his horn-rimmed eyeglass frames. His khaki trousers were rolled up to the knees, and in each hand he carried a ten-pound plastic bag of Italian plums. I remembered being told by an obstetrician that the normal uterus is the size of a small plum. When I asked Dr. Loquesto if this was correct, he said, "No, it's the size of an orange. A mandarin orange, not a navel orange—a juice orange."

"What about those round red plums?" I asked. "I don't know anything about plums," he said. But even when teaching or trying to learn a surgical procedure, the Nantucket surgeon couldn't have needed that many plums. Another time, I saw him standing on a floral-patterned hooked rug in the hospital lobby—this time in rolled-up pants, with gardening dirt all over the knees and bits of earth under his fingernails. When I asked some friends about his appearance, they said that he liked to bake, and garden, too.

I'd also been told that a neighborhood man had to live on intravenous nourishment because one stormy, foggy winter night many years ago he couldn't be flown to Boston and was operated on in Nantucket, where a surgeon felt it best to remove several feet of everything. "You're right near Boston!"

Dr. Loquesto would shout whenever I asked him what if this or that happened while I was under his care. He never had the fog on his mind. "Fog! Very romantic!" he'd yell if I tried to explain the weather conditions.

I knew the man who lived on intravenous fluids because he'd walked around our corner one day and spoken to me for a few minutes. There was nothing unusual-looking about him except his outfit—brand-new-looking blue jeans and blue jean jacket. A white-haired seventy-year-old man in all new blue jeans looked odd. Otherwise he was the picture of health. "He looks fine to me," I said to a seventy-five-year-old neighbor, who'd told me about the surgery. "That's because you didn't see him before," my neighbor said.

As I drove to the coffee-bean store that hot morning nearing noon, I thought of other elderly neighborhood men and of things they had said to me. One of these men also had white hair but more correct trousers, Nantucket reds—not correct-looking to me. They were more like pants a doll would wear. He was discussing the fine day with me when I had the courage to ask him where he'd gotten his eyeglass frames—the kind of clear plastic Socialist-style frames my husband was always breaking. "In New York—a place on Madison Avenue," he said. He suddenly became enlivened by the memory of his purchasing experience and he said, "A bouncy Jewish girl sold them to me." I tried to remove all expression from my face, to prevent him from telling more, but he continued: "I was planning on getting a pair like my old horn-rimmed ones when this bouncy Jewish salesgirl said she thought these would look good." (When I mentioned the incident to a friend who specializes in the interpretation of anti-Semitic slurs, she said that the man was probably in a state of sexual excitement at the time he bought the frames.) I remembered standing in the lane in the sun, listening to him and beginning to feel ill from his description and its implication of how much anti-Semitism there was in the world, in addition to all the other hatreds and evils—from that and from the heat of the rays of the sun without the protection of the giant elms that the early settlers and whaling captains had cut down. After a while the man changed the adjective from "bouncy" to "vivacious," and went on his way.

He was soon distracted by another neighborhood man, who waved to him from across the lane. I recognized this one from his small, round, horn-rimmed frames, his white hair—which he wore parted in the middle—and his clean yellow polo shirt and red-plaid Bermuda shorts. He had a small dog with him and the dog looked just like him except for the hair and outfit. When he stopped, his little dog sat down and waited patiently while the man told me what a good year it was for beach plums and even told me his source of the plentiful crop. "It's a kind of sickness," he went on. "Whenever you see them you have to pick them." I agreed. He said that every day he brought some home and boiled them up until he had enough juice for jelly. I asked if he ever kept them in the refrigerator until he had one big batch, but he said, Hell no, he boiled up a batch each day. I thought of the many sacks of beach plums I kept in the refrigerator, dreading the "picking over" step of the jelly-making process. Then I had so many plums that it took me hours to separate them, trying to discard the imperfect ones, as I'd seen in a fraudulent commercial about some corporate jelly-maker's method. Every summer after that, as the refrigerator filled up with beach plums, I had the memory of this man's puritan jelly-making ethic to compare with mine.

The route to the coffee-bean store was tricky. If you weren't paying attention, you'd miss the turn onto the only street that didn't have a "One Way" sign. Then you'd find a maze where you'd be trapped into driving miles to find a two-way street. During this ride, my headache would get worse, with the sun beating in on all sides of the car. It was illegal to tint a windshield, and Dr. Loquesto's youngest son had advised me not to tint the windows too dark, because the car would look like a drug dealer's car. I'd never seen a drug dealer in a Volvo station wagon but I took his advice.

In the tiny parking lot at the coffee-bean store I found a parking spot in the shade of a tree. I put on my sun hat for the trip across the lot and up the steps to the store. As usual, there was one college-age carpenter or another talking to the college-girl clerks and I didn't want to interrupt and ruin the fun and high expectations of their encounters. I looked over at the periodical rack in the hope that I wouldn't see anything too interesting. Deliveries were delayed by the early-morning fog, so I'd already read everything there. But I wanted to avoid a repeat of the experience where I'd spent fifteen minutes standing in this store, with a bad headache, while reading an article about erotomania in *Star.* Dr. Loquesto had mentioned that he was being pursued by some erotomaniacs. A colleague of his told me, "He's the type who gets the erotomaniacs because of all his power." I couldn't believe it. Still, I'd read the entire article with my head pounding and the sound of the background conversations: "I'm like, 'Should I go windsurfing or should I go rollerblading?' "

When the series of carpenters had left with their cups of coffee and unhealthful snacks—red cherry bread with blueberry cream cheese was one—the cashier told me that they were out of organically grown beans. I paid for the *Times,* and she directed me to the health-food store downtown. I could see that I would be spending most of the day on these coffee beans, because I knew that the health-food store had no grinder. That meant a trip to the gourmet store down the block to ask if they would mind grinding beans purchased elsewhere.

It took an hour to get the beans and have them ground. A sixteen-year-old boy with an earring was the salesman at the health-food store. He was advising an eighteen-year-old boy with a backpack about which soy beverage to buy. They were reading the labels carefully, with the older boy pointing out that his favorite brand had only one percent fat and ten fewer calories per glass than the others. Neither of them liked the nondairy beverage Rice Dream, even though it was made from brown rice.

On my way home I memorized the locations of some lanes with light-pink and light-peach hollyhocks for my planned seed gathering in September. But after a while I saw so many hollyhocks, some planted in the wrong places, that I began to wonder whether they were a good idea after all.

I turned in to our lane. The car still smelled from the ground up, organically grown coffee beans. I took the bag of beans and the *Times* and stepped out into the sun. Then I heard my name being called. Who knew my name in the little neighborhood and would call it out in such a friendly way? I looked across the field and saw that it was a neighbor who was descended from a branch of the English and Scotch-

Irish aristocracy. I hadn't known we were back on speaking terms since the time she'd misinterpreted a complimentary remark I'd made about the renovation of her three-hundred-year-old house.

The truth was that people in the beautiful little neighborhood hated each other. They were on guard, as in a duel—the way we thought in childhood that duellers said to each other before drawing swords, "On guard!"

"I just love this neighborhood," we'd all say to one another. The women would say that. Each man had a reason he'd just as soon live on the cliff, near the sea, or on the moors. I pointed out to my husband that most of the women had had a tiny bit of plastic surgery and looked much better because of it. It proved how prevalent the surgery was getting to be. The only one who'd had more than a bit was eighty-three—she'd had a great deal, plus some special vitamin-and-herb injections at clinics in Switzerland—and she looked best of all. Or maybe her face was just temporarily pinned up to her scalp with paper clips and Scotch tape, since she always wore a wig, and who knew what went on under the wig? This was a use of wigs I'd read about in a fashion magazine.

But it turned out that the neighbor was speaking to me only to inquire about another neighbor. She sure looked great—I couldn't help noticing, and I told her so.

"You do, too," she said.

"Oh, no," I said. "I'm losing the whole thing. But you'll always look good. You have bone structure."

She touched her face and said, "I hope it holds up. It's all I have."

"Of course it will. Bones don't fall in." I'd never heard of osteoporosis of the jaw or cheekbones, and Freud was the only one I knew of who'd had a serious jawbone disease. This woman was into the decade after the forties but still looked better than I did. Her eyes were bluer than mine— they were that light, anti-Semitic blue—and her cheeks were that rosy, anti-Semitic pink. Probably she'd been playing tennis all morning. "I'm off for my swim," she said, explaining a heavy white towel around her neck. I didn't see how she could bear it in the hot sun. Her posture was perfect, and her teeth were white and perfect, too. I pictured her swimming back and forth. That must have been how she kept her excellent muscle tone and circulatory glow. When the conversation was over I was going to look at her legs. She was in her bathing suit, so it would be easy to do.

I was careful not to ask about her husband, because no one had informed me that summer whether he was still alive. "Where is he?" and "Is he still alive?" were two questions that occurred to people every year. To consider either question was to face the passage of time. I wanted to avoid that. Because when I had first spoken to the husband everything was more fun for all of us. I'd heard all about him and her. She was in her forties and he was in his seventies. He was a tall and handsome member of the landed gentry. "He had land deeded to him by the king of England in the sixteen-hundreds" was something people liked to say about him. He'd been married a few times. He had children in their forties. Then, at some point, he and the woman got married and had twin girls.

One year, before I'd ever seen the husband, I spoke to him on the phone about renting their guest cottage. In discussing the number of bedrooms, he asked, "Do you have children?" and I said, "No, I'm going to wait until I'm forty."

"Oh, don't do that," he said. "You'll have to have your tubes blown and all. It's no fun." He went on to repeat his age and the age of his blue-eyed wife, and to mention various medical procedures they'd gone through in attempting to have a child. And all I wanted was to rent their little guest cottage. The blowing of the tubes was something I couldn't get off my mind. Luckily, I never met the man after the conversation but just saw him from a distance. My husband would comment on his handsomeness, saying that he looked like Douglas Fairbanks, Jr., or Howard Hughes.

It turned out that the man was still alive and was staying in their home in another historic part of Massachusetts, maybe on the land the king had deeded to him. He had around-the-clock care, but his wife had to be in Nantucket for the sake of the twin girls. As I was imagining the situation, I remembered seeing the little girls tackling the man around his handsome head about eight years before.

Now his condition was not that good, she said. She described his symptoms of confusion and memory loss. "Then there's the sleeping," she said.

I thought of my father and his symptoms. The symptoms sounded the same. "Sleeping—is that a sign?" I asked.

"Oh, yes. You have to watch for that. That's a sign. That's what we had. Sleep, sleep, sleep. I'd find him sleeping in the garden."

It didn't sound that bad to me. Especially the way she said the words. She had so much expression in her voice as she described the symptoms and repeated the word "sleep." She had a certain rhythm with the words—it sounded in between Dylan Thomas and James Joyce. Sometimes everything the Irish said sounded like a poem.

"Yes, we'd find him lying down and sleeping in the garden. That was it. Yes—sleep, sleep, sleep in the garden."

I tried to imagine the garden. Did it have a rose-covered arbor? Was there wisteria growing over the garden gate? Were there peach and pink hollyhocks planted alongside the white fence? Or was it all green, just a big, all-green garden of grass, evergreens, moss, and ferns? An all-green garden sounded like a better place to sleep than one filled with flowers, even if the petals were light colors, or all white. The colors and shapes of the flowers might be a distraction from lying down and sleeping. You'd be wanting to keep your eyes open for one more look.

The man was tall. I pictured him lying down and folding himself up in the garden to sleep. He seemed happy there. But then I pictured my father, old and alone, folding himself into the same position and sleeping in his bed at night. This was something I thought about when I tried to fall asleep. It would keep me awake for a while or most of the night.

The sight of my neighbor standing in the sun with the heavy towel around her neck took my mind off my own problems and made me wish she would leave for her long swim.

"You must come by and see the house when I've got it together," she said.

"I'm sure it's beautiful," I said. "It looks good from the outside."

I knew the house was crooked and had wide, crooked, seventeenth-century floorboards. I hoped they'd left it that way. I hoped it was the same as when I'd first been inside it.

Then she waved good-bye and took off. I remembered to look at her legs. They looked like the legs of a very young woman. Everything was in place, and I knew that there was no way to pull up leg skin and muscle with clips or tape under a bathing suit, even though I no longer read fashion magazines. It turned out that what I'd read in *Vogue* when I was twelve—"The hours from noon to two are the best for suntanning"—was bad advice.

Back in our house, I lay down on a wicker chaise in front of an electric fan and drank one cup of black coffee while looking at a photograph of the President in the *Times*. If he had such brilliant advisers, why didn't they advise him to stop blow-drying his hair? There was no mention of the subject in the newspaper.

After reading about his troubles and his bad diet I noticed that my headache was cured. I decided to look for *Bartlett's Familiar Quotations* and see if I could find that poem about the heart leaping. I remembered no reference books in the entire house and only the Fannie Farmer cookbook to refer to for jelly-making techniques. It was too hot to go to the library in town, and most of my neighbors were illiterate, though fine neighbors in every other way. The only literate person I knew in Massachusetts, where the phone rates were low enough to call during the day, was Dr. Loquesto's twelve-year-old son. He'd recently called me and said, "I find Clinton's hair so disturbing." The two of them, father and son, had a big library and were always looking things up. Some of their books were in the surgeon's study and others were in the library. Would it be an imposition on the boy to ask him to look up a poem in a book?

He'd once showed me the system he'd used for separating his father's books into different rooms. "The medical books are in his study," the boy said. "How about this one?" I asked, pointing to a medical textbook in their library. "He doesn't do diseases—he'd only look at that once in five years," the boy said. "What about this psychology textbook?" I asked. "I guess he'd never use it." I said.

"He thinks he knows all he needs to about psychology," he said. Then he smiled.

If the boy was able to find the poem, he'd have to read it out loud on the phone. I knew that he'd read it in a cynical way. I remembered what the surgeon had said against Surrealism when he thought he'd seen some in my photographs. "I like Realism, I like Romanticism, I'm too busy for Surrealism!" he yelled. But if he liked Romanticism, why wouldn't he look out the window at the sky when the sun was setting? Even when he was passing right by a window he refused to look. The truth must have been that he hated Romanticism. Probably he didn't even know what the word meant when he yelled out that he liked it.

I decided to call the surgeon's son anyway. He usually came through with the information I needed. He sounded as if he was laughing when he answered the phone. When I asked what he was doing he said, "Looking through the medicine cabinet."

"What could be funny in there?" I asked.

"I found a bottle of hydrogen peroxide with the expiration date 1976," he said.

Immediately I thought better of asking him to look up the poem. One reason was that his heart didn't leap up for anything. If it did, he kept it hidden. This would cause him problems later on. Also, he hadn't completed the last assignment I'd given him: "When in Wellesley the next time, please find

Anne Sexton's childhood home and report to me on what it looks like." I needed this information for my plan to photograph three of the poet's houses in Massachusetts. But the boy wasn't interested. "I know where Thoreau's house is," he said.

I decided to wait until dark and go to the bookstore to find the quote. I'd follow my usual plan for the middle of the day—until the light turned right for photographing the moors and ponds I was interested in. I'd read the *Times,* checking for signs of hope. I'd deadhead the perennials and the fairy roses. I'd go to the beach at four. I'd sit under the umbrella and read the parts of the *Times* I'd skipped. When most people left the beach, I'd go swimming, I'd work on removing the polo player from some bathing trunks I'd bought for my husband, I'd go to three farms to find the best corn. I thought about what I'd read in the obituary of the Nobel Prize geneticist Barbara McClintock: "She spent her life working on corn." Then I'd go home and take another shower and put on more mascara. I'd take my camera in my bicycle basket and go for a long ride. On the ride I'd stop and take the photographs I'd been waiting for. On the way back, it would be cool and dark enough to go to the bookstore.

The reference section of the bookstore wasn't popular. No section was popular at that hour, because people were home having their dinners—big platters of corn. I had the whole store to myself. If I found the quote I'd buy the book.

I quickly found the word "Heart." On the way to "Heart" from the back of the book I saw "Wisdom," "Wish," "Sorrows," and "Soul," "Sigh," "Shudders," "Seas," and "Secure."

The Magic Flute was playing on the stereo. I felt some euphoria coming on. When I had more time, I'd read this whole book and everything quoted in it, even though the plan sounded like something a hostage in Iran might do to pass the hours. I was momentarily distracted by "Heartstrings are a lute." Why hadn't I read more poetry? Another way I had wasted my life occurred to me. "My heart is pure," "my heart is sick and sad," "my heart is heavy," "my heart is at rest," "I am sick at heart," and nothing about "my heart-rate target zone during aerobic activity"—the way the word is used now.

There it was. "My heart leaps up."

My heart leaps up when I behold
A rainbow in the sky.

But my heart quickly fell back down when I remembered this famous poem and realized that my education was so poor that I had forgotten it.

I'd buy all of Wordsworth's poems. I'd buy some Keats, too, and a scholarly work on the Romantic poets. I would read Spenser's *Faerie Queene*. If Keats liked it so much, it had to be good. I went to the Wordsworth shelf. Right on the same page with "My Heart Leaps Up" was "To a Butterfly." With the headache and the blow-drying of the President's hair and the reading of the *Times* and the watching of "Crossfire," I'd forgotten about the Romantic poets.

Maybe my life as a wastrel in the garden looking at white butterflies wasn't a crime. I'd try to overlook the part of Wordsworth's life where "he finally set up house with his beloved sister." I wouldn't blame myself for forgetting the poem. Because when I'd phoned an English waiter from a Tuscan restaurant in Southampton to offer him a quince tree we were digging up, "Somewhere over the rainbow" was playing in the background on his answering machine.

I tried to picture a rainbow and remember the last time I'd seen one. It was a few years ago, right there on Nantucket, up near the cliff. I was riding my bike. A little boy called to me, "Look!" as he pointed to the sky. Since I was still fresh from city life I thought he was pointing out something I should beware of. And as I looked around, I saw nothing menacing or anything at all. The boy kept pointing and called, "Don't you see it?"

"See what?" I said. "What is it?"

"A rainbow," the boy said.

And then I did see it. It was a faint rainbow separated in the middle by what was left of the blue of the sky. I thanked the boy, and he said, "Yup," and kept walking.

I remembered that as a time when my heart leapt up. I was glad to be on an island where a child would point out a rainbow to a stranger, even though the grown-ups of the island resorted to plastic surgery, described reproductive surgery, straightened crooked floors, and admired George Bush. Except for our favorite neighbors, who were mad at the Pope and disgusted with Republicans. I'd read in an encyclopedia that "for Percy Bysshe Shelley there was no distinction between poetry and politics," whatever that meant. Maybe if I read the Romantic poets and worshiped nature along with Wordsworth, and the President became a vegetarian, my heart would leap up again. Probably not. Not as high up—I was sure of that.

I Couldn't See a Thing

For three years, I'd been trying to photograph the world-renowned reproductive surgeon Dr. Arnold Loquesto. After benefiting from his surgical skills, I'd followed him around New England and New York to conferences and hospitals where he lectured. I'd met and photographed everyone in his family and in his office. But it turned out that the surgeon couldn't stay still long enough for the right photograph to be taken.

I began to think of these trips as a form of research, after reading in an antique photography book in the chapter on small mammals, "Know your subject. Otherwise many opportunities will be entirely lost."

The first time I traveled from East Hampton to Massachusetts for a photograph, I found the surgeon sitting on a little swivel chair in front of a screen where he was arranging some slides. He didn't even swivel around to acknowledge my arrival, but said to the screen, "What's new?" I got the idea to take a picture of the back of his neck and head, but I thought it would have a surreal, Magritte look I wasn't aiming for.

"What's on the slides?" I asked.

"Weddings and and other celebrations. I'm starting a band and renting it out to make extra money at big events."

I looked at the screen and saw some surgical shots.

"Endometriosis. You love this kind of thing," he said.

As he prepared his slides for a lecture he was going to give in New York, he sat on the chair and described some of the bar-mitzvah celebrations he'd attended. "One was an Egyptian feast," he said, still staring at the screen as I tried to photograph him with the endometriomas lit up dark-red on the white screen before him.

"Is that appropriate?" I asked.

"Everybody loved it," he said. "Except for one man, a dermatologist whose specialty is suspicious-looking lesions."

"Could I get an appointment with him?" I asked. "I always think I have the most dangerous kind."

"You're not a candidate for melanoma," he said. "Because you're so pale."

"I thought that's what makes a candidate," I said.

"You never go in the sun," he said.

"It's sun from the past," I told him. But he didn't understand. Because the surgeon had a kind of dyslexia of his thought patterns which made him think in reverse. Based on my observations of his mental processes and also on a patient's telling me that he had written her instructions backward, I decided to ask him, "By the way, do you have dyslexia?"

He had moved over to his large desk. He was reading some mail and wasn't paying attention to the question but answered, "Huh? Yes. I think I do. Why?" That gave me the courage to start preparing the other question I'd been wanting to ask.

"Has your wife ever had shock therapy?" That might make him look up from his mail and say, "Why?"

Then all I could say would be, "Just wondering."

I knew I had to wait for the right moment to ask that. Actually, I didn't want to know the answer. I might never ask. Because the more I saw of the surgeon the more I understood that his behavior would have been enough to cause the shocked expressions his wife and children had sometimes.

At the end of the day a resident met us outside to drive us to a meeting of doctors who were going to discuss articles from medical textbooks. The surgeon sat alone in the back of the car and I sat next to the resident in the front. "I hope they started without us," the surgeon said. "They probably didn't—the idiots."

I turned around to look at him. He was wearing a light-blue-and-yellow Argyle vest, which seemed to take up the whole back seat. The diamonds were stretched out of shape by his abdominal area. He had a Humpty-Dumpty look about him.

"When did you develop your contempt for mankind?" I asked him.

"Very early," the surgeon said.

"Thirteen?" I asked.

"Earlier."

"Seven?"

"Earlier."

"Five?"

"Yes. Five," he said.

As we passed a neighborhood of old mansions the surgeon said, "I want to live here."

I'd been hoping to photograph him in front of the Frick Museum, because he'd once said he wished he could live there, too. This was to be part of a series of photographs of people with houses they wished they could live in. "The Frick is better than these houses," I said. "But it costs six million dollars for an apartment overlooking the Frick Museum."

"I can handle it," he said. "I'll do a few D and Cs."

"You mean a few hundred thousand," I said.

"As many as I have to in order to pay the rent."

"What's your favorite surgery?" I asked.

"Hysterectomy!" he yelled.

"What's the reason?" I asked.

"Cut out the uterus. Throw it in a pot."

"What kind of pot do they throw it into?" I asked. I wanted to know.

"A big bucket," the surgeon said in a deep, low voice.

He'd gotten into the mood to ridicule critics of his profession, even though they admired him for his new surgical techniques for preventing hysterectomies, and his low fees, too.

The next month I attended the lecture and slide show that the surgeon had been preparing. It was at the hospital I knew to be one of the two cruelest in New York. The kind of camera I needed to photograph in the dark auditorium wasn't allowed in there. I remembered the advice in the photography book in the chapter on larger animals: "No pursuit contains more disappointments and none requires a greater amount of patience. It is no unusual thing to work a whole day, to be forced to quit at nightfall with no results to show."

I'd learned from my past experiences with the hospital that all the male doctors had white hair and red faces. Little did they know that the very slides they'd assembled to watch had been prepared during a description of something Hebrew. They wore white coats and resembled the German-style butchers from Yorkville who sell knockwurst and other kinds of wurst. One of the white-haired, white-coated doctors sat in an aisle seat in the large auditorium while practicing his golf swing and ignoring the lecture. After a few swings with his imaginary golf club, he and his colleagues passed rolls of colored Life Savers back and forth. Probably they'd muttered anti-Semitic comments about Dr. Loquesto before the lecture or would do so afterwards. But the surgeon's Italian name might have confused the doctors and kept them from knowing which kind of slur to make.

My next trip took place on a perfect day in June. I left a garden where I'd been photographing white roses and traveled across Long Island to a highway restaurant where the surgeon was giving another slide show for a hundred doctors. It had been difficult to get permission to photograph the surgeon at this event. "They're a strange group," he said.

I had to describe my project by telephone to a secretary who sounded like Little Richard. As I was telling her my plans she suddenly said, "Ooooh!" I was surprised that she was impressed. Then she said, "Oooh! oooh! oooh!" and added, "The reason I'm saying 'oooh' like that is because a big hornet just flew in the window."

When I arrived at the restaurant, right at an exit off the Long Island Expressway, the doctors were standing around drinking soda and talking to each other. None of them had met Dr. Loquesto before. The surgeon stood by himself for a few minutes, and then went to arrange the slides. He put his briefcase down on the fake bricks of a giant fake hearth, opened it up, and sat down. He looked the way Fuller Brush men used to look when they came into houses and had to take out their samples wherever they could.

As I was trying to photograph this sight, the secretary came over to me and said in Little Richard's voice, "This isn't the kind of picture we thought you wanted to take."

"I don't mind," the surgeon said without looking up.

After the lecture was over and linguine had been served as a first course, the surgeon said he couldn't wait much longer. "Three more minutes," he said, looking at his watch. The president of the doctors said, "You don't have to wait for the second course."

The surgeon was still staring at his watch. "That's it!" he said all of a sudden, and he jumped out of his seat. He grabbed his briefcase from the hearth and ran up the stairs. I followed him out to the parking lot, where a long white limousine was waiting. It was part of my plan to photograph the surgeon in front of an airport hotel where he had to meet forty other doctors who were spending the night before flying off to another meeting. I'd been told by the secretary that the car was for Dr. Loquesto and I was forbidden to ride with him. But when I told this to the surgeon he said, "What do they care? Just get in."

On the way to the airport Dr. Loquesto announced that he was moving to a hospital near Boston.

"I wish you had told me the news more gradually," I said.

"Why? All my patients are free to follow me there."

I didn't know what he meant, because two of his favorite jokes were: "I have all the nut cases here" and "All our patients are neurotic."

The limousine driver got lost on the Expressway. I kept calling directions to him, "Grand Central to La Guardia," but the limousine was so long that he couldn't hear. By the time we arrived, the forty doctors had gone to their forty rooms. Instead of asking them to come down, I took a photograph of the surgeon checking in by himself in the lobby.

The week after the restaurant slide show, the surgeon broke the news that he was moving to a wooded suburb near Concord. The first thing I thought of was that Anne Sexton had lived right nearby. Because after reading her poems and her biography, all I wanted to do was stare at and photograph her houses. I didn't see how poems could be written in suburbs. When I read the descriptions of her houses, I tried to picture her in them. I wondered how anyone could turn into a poet under the circumstances of her life.

That was how I got the brainstorm: When I'm in Massachusetts to photograph the surgeon, I'll photograph Anne Sexton's houses, too! First the home of her early childhood, in Wellesley; next, the home of her teenage years, in Weston; and then another house in Weston, where she lived when she was a poet. I decided to skip her house in Newton, because I'd been to Newton and knew that it was filled with dentists and lawyers.

One of her houses had tall windows and a sunporch. There were trees and gardens. Another had seven bathrooms, a playroom, and a library. How could you be mentally disturbed in a house like that, I wondered stupidly. People were lucky to have lived in bygone eras, I thought, even though they're dead now.

I told the surgeon's twelve-year-old son about my plan. I'd gotten to know him on the occasions when the surgeon tried to foist off the photography sessions on his son. "Take his picture today instead," he'd say.

I gave the boy the addresses of the houses and asked him to go by when he was in the neighborhood and give me a report. Then I told the surgeon that Anne Sexton's houses were near his new home.

"That's the first thing I've heard to make me glad I'm moving there," he said. "I wanted to live in Beacon Hill."

But he hadn't read any of her poems, and knew nothing about her life except for a few salacious bits that he liked to yell out whenever her name was mentioned. I sent him the volume that included an ode to the uterus, because I once heard him shout to a patient, "No more uterine questions!" as he boarded a hospital elevator filled with a bunch of doctors and nurses. I thought that when he read the poem he'd prefer the questions.

"What if Anne Sexton had been your patient?" I asked him after I pointed out the ode. He didn't answer.

A few months went by. In the fall, Dr. Loquesto moved to the suburb. Every time I went to photograph him at his new hospital that winter, I'd think about how close I was to the three houses and to Walden Pond. But I could never fit the surgeon and the houses and pond into the same day; I'd get involved watching the surgeon's activities. I'd read in the photography book, "One cannot afford to miss the details that go to make a truthful whole in depicting incidents in the everyday lives of birds and beasts."

Then, just when I was making plans to photograph the surgeon standing next to a special telescope he liked to use, he suggested that I come up for a medical procedure with the telescope. Immediately I thought of combining the medical appointment with the plan to photograph Anne Sexton's houses. I decided I had to go to Boston in June in spite of what could happen with the greenhouse effect.

The night before the trip I lay in bed reviewing my plan. I was happy. But there was no reason for it. I thought over my situation in a quick way: I had electrodes on my chest to monitor a fluttering heartbeat; the portable monitor was on the floor on a pile of books near the bed; in the pile were Nietzsche, Keats, and Raymond Carver. Maybe this combination caused the arrhythmia.

On the bedside table there was half a cup of chamomile tea with a teaspoon of valerian-root tincture mixed in. The table was as cluttered with bottles, cups, and glasses as Marilyn Monroe's bedside table at the time of her suspicious death. But I had no immediate plans to commit suicide. Nor did I have a fear of being murdered by Mafia hit men sent by any of the remaining Kennedys.

I'd take the three ferries to New London. The hotel driver would meet me and drive the two hours to Boston. It was a professional expenditure and a once-in-a-lifetime occurrence. I'd get out of the air-conditioned car and go right into the air-conditioned hotel. Soon I'd be in a room overlooking the Public Garden. The next day, just before the medical procedure, I'd take a Demerol and a Xanax. Afterward, it wouldn't be a good idea to get right back onto the highway and the three ferries, so I'd recover at the hotel, and then— off to the three houses. On the way there, I could stop by and see how the surgeon's house looked in daylight. In a photograph I'd seen, the house looked like the Guggenheim Museum. It was made of white stone and faced a big pond.

In fact, when I got through with the series of the surgeon and of Anne Sexton's houses I planned to return to nature—to ponds in particular. I'd never even been to Walden Pond. An antique postcard of a pond in Nantucket—"Sunset over Sesachacha Pond"—had led to my fascination with the subject. I wanted to see this pond at all hours and photograph it in every kind of light. Then one pond led to another.

After ponds, I was going to move on to bogs and heathlands, if there were any left. Maybe all the photographs could be connected at the end—the surgeon standing near the pond outside his big house, then his youngest son at Walden Pond. First the people, then the ponds, then the people with the ponds. The boy was planning to start a conservative Republican club at his school, and he was against preservation and ecology. He didn't know that the Republicans had cornered for themselves the most beautiful, best-preserved parts of America, with golf courses included. Or maybe he did.

In the past, after weeks of studying ponds in Southampton, East Hampton, and Nantucket, I'd think of the surgeon and his family. They'd pop into my mind as a diversion, the way my dollhouse would during my childhood. The surgeon's wife looked like the mother in the dollhouse family. Their kitchen cabinets held the same groceries as the miniatures in the dollhouse—cans of La Choy Chop Suey and bottles of Wish-Bone salad dressing. Their favorite dressing was white, and was made by mixing three kinds of supermarket dressings together. But there was no doll in the dollhouse collection that resembled the surgeon.

My plan still seemed like a great idea the next day. As I took the two five-minute ferries to get to the one-and-a-half-hour ferry that crossed Long Island Sound, I remembered reading that Anne Sexton had taken the Cross Sound Ferry in the opposite direction to get to a poetry conference in Montauk. But her trips were more fun than mine, always combining love affairs and drinking bouts with whatever work she was doing. Actually, it didn't sound like fun when I thought about it.

I arrived at the hotel late at night. It was my favorite hotel in Boston and the hotel where Anne had hung out—in the bar with other intoxicated poets. I remembered staying in the hotel room before, with my husband, waiting for the right day to meet Dr. Loquesto in his laboratory when he first moved to Massachusetts. I saw how desolate it was to be alone in a hotel room in a strange city, even though the hotel had been built in 1927 and had a view of the Public Garden and gave out Mountain Valley water in green glass bottles.

I lay down on the hotel bed and turned on CNN. I lined up my herbal sleeping tinctures and teas, and took out my noise-blocking sound machine. Then I unpacked some clothes and put them out on chairs around the room. The room didn't get any cheerier. Hotel rooms don't grow cheery just because your belongings are strewn about. I thought of Dr. Loquesto's skills in packing and traveling. "I pack brown or I pack blue," he'd told me when I first met him and asked how he managed all the packing for his medical forays around the world.

I thought of the surgeon unpacking his brown or blue garments and putting them away in neat stacks in his hotel dresser drawers. His wife had once invited me up to see their accommodations in a city I traveled to in order to photograph a dinner dance of ninety-five reproductive surgeons. "How do you know what's been in those drawers?" I asked them. "I have to unpack—what can I do?" he said. He took out his toiletry kit. All it contained was a beat-up black plastic razor, a small black comb missing half its plastic teeth, a tiny squeezed-out tube of toothpaste, and a small worn-out toothbrush. I watched the surgeon take out and line up the items of his kit, and I thought he might have a moment of recognition of the sadness of these things as he gazed at them with a forlorn stare. Maybe I could send him a new shaving kit as a present for some occasion. Patients and other people were always sending him presents. I'd seen hundreds of champagne and wine bottles covered with dust in their places on shelves in his basement.

The spell of the sadness of the surgeon's toiletry kit was broken by his wife's saying, "Let's go see the different kinds of marble they used in the shower."

Instead of dreading the medical procedure with Dr. Loquesto, I was looking forward to it as I watched CNN in my hotel room. Because I still hoped that someday I could photograph him with the special telescope he used, but so far I was afraid to see what it looked like. Usually I was so distracted by the surgeon's behavior that I forgot about whatever procedure he was doing. Some patients told me that they chose to do without medication or anesthesia. Others said they were never offered any. In the recovery room after surgery, when nurses suggested drugs like morphine, the surgeon would yell, "All they need is Tylenol!"

The next day I took the two drugs. I quickly found that I could hardly walk. In the elevator I had to lean on the back wall. I wondered why people enjoy being drug addicts.

The first taxi in the line in front of the hotel was driven by a man I thought I recognized as a Libyan terrorist. On top of that, he needed directions to get to the medical building, which was ten blocks away. But, even in a fully conscious state, I can't give directions in strange cities. This caused a delay.

"You just missed Dr. Loquesto," the nurse said. "As you arrived in one elevator, he left in the other one."

"I'm only five minutes late."

"Usually we're all waiting for him. I'll go call him," she said.

She pointed me to a waiting room filled with magazines about decorating. In order to avoid this room, I told her about my drugged state.

"O.K.," she said. "Better wait in a real room."

After I'd waited awhile in a room filled with medical equipment, she called me to the phone.

"What do you want?" Dr. Loquesto shouted into the phone. "You stayed over—how could you be late?"

I explained how.

"Today I was there on time," he said. I could hear him breathing through the phone. I imagined the smoke that pours out of dragons' heads.

"I can come back later," I said.

"I'm busy later. This isn't a necessary test anyway. I only do it when patients are neurotic."

"You said all the patients were neurotics."

"That's right. Those are the ones who get this test."

When the surgeon arrived in another hour, the high point of the drug combination had worn off. As he prepared the telescope and talked in a loud voice about his ruined schedule, I tried to think myself back to the drugged feeling. I was listening to *The Magic Flute* on my Walkman, and it wasn't right for the occasion. But the sound of the magic bells in Act I and the thought of finally getting to photograph Anne Sexton's houses, combined with the background of the doctor's angry muttering, had a transcendental effect.

What did it matter how the surgeon behaved? The three houses were all that counted. Then I got the idea that the surgeon could play the part of Papageno in an all-surgeon production of *The Magic Flute.* Why hadn't I thought of this before? Perhaps Dr. Loquesto was a descendant of the librettist Emanuel Schikaneder, who died in 1812 after ten years of insanity.

When I got back to the hotel, I lay down on the bed and looked out the window at the Public Garden and the ruined skyline in the background. I was beginning to feel that this room was my home. The hotel staff was nicer to me than anyone in any home I'd ever lived in. The idea, I understood in what remained of my drug-expanded consciousness, was this: People could be trained and paid to be kind to you.

I called the surgeon's wife to tell her I would be passing through her neighborhood. Summer vacation had started at the school where she taught a course on musicals of the nineteen-fifties. She had told me that she wanted to go along to see Anne Sexton's houses, but after I gave a brief description, she said that she had to wait for an ottoman to be delivered. "Why don't you stop by and see our house instead?" she said. "Maybe the ottoman will be here, and you can see that, too."

The concierge arranged for a car to come and drive me to the three houses. The clean blond driver acted as though anyone who would pay for this service should be treated with courtesy and respect. I wasn't used to that. He jumped out of

the car and opened the door for me. I got in. The air conditioner was going. Immediately I started to have fun. I forgot
my troubles. It was possible that I had some remaining euphoria from the Demerol. Maybe I could take a permanent room
at this hotel. The surgeon's wife had told me that a count lived
there.

Dr. Loquesto's wife and dog greeted me at the door. The
dog started his jumping. When the jumping got out of control, I heard the surgeon's wife use a curse word. Not that I
blamed her. It was certainly called for by the situation. But
she was looking like that doll from my dollhouse, so the word
didn't fit.

The surgeon's eighteen-year-old son was there. As usual,
the twelve-year-old boy was wandering around his large
house, from one odd pursuit to another. He was reading a cat-
alogue for wealthy middle-aged men and planning to order a
few things.

We went outside and sat down on some lawn furniture. I
looked around the property and got some landscaping ideas.
But then I noticed that the surgeon's wife was wearing nylon
stockings. You couldn't garden in those. With a garden, you
had to be ready to rush into it at any time to deadhead a
flower or pull out a weed.

The dog had joined us and was sitting down.

"What's wrong with him?" the older son asked his mother.

"He ate some poison. That's why he's drooling. The vet
did something, but it didn't work."

"Maybe he needs to go back," the son said.

"This is why we don't have a dog," I said.

"Why?" the son said. "You get them cured, and then it's
fun again."

I'd never thought of that. I forgot that things can get better. I thought things could only get worse. This is why it's important to go out into the world and not stay alone with ponds. People tell you things.

"I'll go call the vet again," the surgeon's wife said as she went into the house.

"I should be going," I said to the son. "I don't want your father to find me here. I was five minutes late for an appointment today."

"Whatever happened, he's forgotten it by now," he said.

"But if he sees me he might remember."

"What do you think it feels like to be one of his children?" he asked.

"You must feel the way Kafka felt," I said.

"How did he feel?"

"He had that situation with his father. I don't think he had a dog."

"Oh, now I remember. I didn't connect it with my own life."

I took off my sunglasses as we went into the house. The dog followed us and started his jumping again. "He's licking my glasses," I said.

"He licks everything," the surgeon's wife said, looking at the animal with a blank expression.

The driver was taking in the early-evening air. He walked around to open the car door for me.

As we drove through hundreds of trees heavy with hanging branches of green leaves, I began to wonder what it was like to live around there. Maybe it was no better than Connect-icut—trees and woods and big old houses. Maybe there was that feeling of nothingness in all suburbs. Emptiness and nothingness. Everything you wanted to go to was somewhere else. The driver stopped in front of a detour marked off with a wooden barricade. "Just when I think I have the answer, obstacles are put in my path," he said.

It wasn't that light out anymore. At last some numbers appeared. "This is it," the driver said. I looked out toward a small hill. The house looked so new, it could have been built in 1973. I saw some modern windows and modern curtains but I couldn't see the screened veranda or the playroom with a garden entrance I'd read about. The place didn't look big enough to have seven bathrooms. It might be the wrong house.

It was easier to find the childhood home in Wellesley. At least it looked old. Maybe it was for sale. I saw myself moving in and living the rest of my life in the tree-filled town. Until that day, I had loved trees. I was like Joyce Kilmer in this respect. But I loved trees where you could see the rest of what's around—sky, clouds, birds, and beyond. Open and flat, with lots of trees at the edges of the flatness. It was getting dark out, and leaves and branches were everywhere. Out the car window to the left I could see a room with tall windows. Maybe it was Anne's childhood bedroom, but there wasn't enough light to take a photograph.

We drove off into the disappearing light to get back to Weston. "O.K.—Black Oak Road," the driver said, driving right up the road. I couldn't see a thing. It was just a black road with some ranch houses. I felt sorrier for Anne than ever. I had an even higher opinion of her. Not that anyone cared what my opinion of Anne Sexton was, or what her houses looked like, either. I looked at the house, a two-story ranch house with black shutters. "There's the pool," the driver said. This couldn't be one of the pools Anne was criticized for building with her poetry earnings. It was a tiny pool. I didn't want to think of her swimming in this sad-looking pool or living in this house. How could you write a poem in such a house? How could you do anything but go crazy? I felt that I was going to go crazy just looking at it.

The next morning, the surgeon's wife called to say that she had an appointment near the hotel and could come up for a minute to see the room. Seeing each other's hotel rooms had got to be part of the project.

As soon as she came in I led her to the window to see the Public Garden.

"What a view," she said. Then she looked at the flowers and fruit the hotel staff had put in the room. "Really lovely," she said.

"Why don't you take it all?" I said. "I can't drag fruit and flowers on three ferries."

We loaded up a plastic hotel bag with the fruit. We put the flowers—big pink peonies—into another bag.

"How about the soap and all that stuff?" I asked. I had my own all-vegetable soap and shampoo.

"If you don't want it." We put the soap in with the flowers. She said the surgeon brought soap from hotels around the world.

"That's thoughtful of him," I said.

"He's just trying to save money," she said.

We went out to the street to wait for her car to come from the hotel garage. A breeze was blowing, even though it was June. Then she asked, "Did you accomplish everything?"

"Some of the things. I shouldn't combine medical appointments with photography projects."

"Not when you have this doctor," she said, staring straight ahead.

"I wish I understood his personality. What's the key?" I said. There was a chance that if I waited with her and missed the ferry I'd find out the secret. I remembered asking her twelve-year-old son how to understand the surgeon's behavior. "No one knows," he said.

We stood and watched the hotel guests coming and going. Every now and then we'd look at each other when an important sentence came up. Looking at the surgeon's wife when she said a sentence about him was as hard as looking at the last house Anne Sexton had lived in. To look at her face and try to take in any information gave me that feeling of going insane again. How could anyone live with the surgeon and how could Anne Sexton have written any poems in that house were two questions I couldn't get out of my head.

"He's a count," the surgeon's wife said out of nowhere. She had a beatific expression on her face.

"A count?" I said. Maybe she meant the surgeon thought of himself as nobility. But from her expression I knew she couldn't be speaking about her husband.

"That man," she said. "That man getting out of the limousine. That's the count who lives at the hotel."

I looked across the street and saw a white-haired man who looked like a waiter in an Italian restaurant. She seemed happy to be seeing the count. She must have just liked the idea of royalty. As a break from her suburban, wooded domain she must have liked to think there was another kind of life, free of poisoned, drooling dogs who needed to be driven to vets, a life free of dinner dances with reproductive surgeons, free of mixing together three kinds of bottled salad dressings, and packing brown or blue for the temperamental surgeon who brought home tiny bars of soap from around the world.

At last her car came. It was a black Alfa Romeo. We loaded in the bags of fruit, flowers, and soap. "Bye," the surgeon's wife called. It sounded like a voice on an answering machine.

I ran into the lobby to ask the desk clerk to get my bill ready. She was busy talking to the white-haired man. "Here's your mail, Count," she said, with a bit of impatience. Why didn't she say Count Something? Maybe his name couldn't be pronounced, so they settled on simply "Count." If you lived there the staff might lose patience after a while. What life did the count have just hanging around Boston in that hotel?

I knew I'd have to come back up there one more time. I thought that after the leaves fell I'd have a better view of the three houses. Maybe the surgeon's house and pond, too. But if I went in winter I'd have to time it just right. Because I wouldn't want to leave East Hampton if there was a full moon and the ponds froze and snow fell on the frozen ponds. I'd want to stay and photograph them. I'd be torn between this pond and that. And I still hadn't been to Walden Pond. I couldn't be everywhere at once.

THE WORLD OF IDEAS

It was the summer I stopped having fun. We were on vacation in our favorite place. A boy came into our kitchen and said, "My mother wants you to come over. She has an emergency about tomatoes." It was nearing the brightest part of the day in my opinion—noon—but I guessed I could manage to go a few yards across the lane to their house. I'd gone down the lane twenty years before to visit the birthplace and observatory of the first woman astronomer, Maria Mitchell, and I'd been trying to go back ever since. It was always too hot during visiting hours, and just when it cooled off, at four o'clock, the hours were over.

"She bought all these tomatoes from one farmer and they're not good and she bought just a few from the other farmer and they're the good ones," the boy said. "She wants you to taste one of each."

But I had just finished drinking macrobiotic twig tea, and I wasn't ready for tomatoes. I explained this to the boy. He was nine.

"Why can't you eat tomatoes after tea?" he asked.

"I'll go over and look at them," I said. I never minded going to their house, since it was so much better in every way than the one we rented. But I had a fear of going over there, too.

We went across the lane up the hill under the apple tree into their kitchen. Everything was custom-made for the Sub-Zero everything else. I didn't want to own Sub-Zero refrigerators but I liked seeing them in other people's kitchens. I wanted an old round-cornered refrigerator from the nineteen-fifties. Although those refrigerators brought back memories of all the animal products I couldn't stand to eat—meat, chicken, milk, and eggs—it was the outside I planned to look at.

When I go into other people's houses I'm like a visitor from another planet looking at the Sub-Zero things they have. "They're not so hot," this tomato woman had said when I admired the tremendous size. "I'm sorry I got them." Among her residences, she had several. And at the home of Dr. Arnold Loquesto, the world-renowned reproductive surgeon I'd consulted and photographed, his wife had said that their Sub-Zero refrigerator wasn't wide enough. This is why it's best not to get into the appliance world too far—you're always disappointed—and also why I'm still waiting for the sandblaster to send someone to take apart our nineteen-thirties stove so he can sandblast it back to its original state of cleanliness.

The boy's mother was in a hyped-up state. I'd recently realized that this was her everyday condition.

"Oh, you came, thank you!" she said. "Only you can understand how distraught I am over these tomatoes."

She was wearing a kind of exercise pants I'd never understood. They were shiny black nylon pedal-pusher-length pants. Why wear anything like that on these hot summer days, or any day? Maybe they conditioned her muscle tone, which was superior to mine. My exercise attire consisted of a man's sleeveless white undershirt and cotton boxer shorts in the pink-and-white-striped pattern Dr. Loquesto had shown to some semiconscious patients in the recovery room. He'd turned around in a modest way, his back to us, and showed us an inch of stripes after one of the patients' husbands had asked about the waistband showing above the surgical bottoms, which were slipping down. The surgeon was trying to blow bubbles with some chewed-out gum but took the time to stop and share his sources for striped shorts and Argyle socks.

As my neighbor worried about the tomatoes, she opened a jar of mayonnaise and put some into a bowl with lobster salad. She was preparing lunch, still dressed in the tight exercise pants. I felt so much more sensibly dressed, in an old thin linen shirt and skirt. I hoped her husband wouldn't come in and ask me why I wore the same shirt every day. I'd already told him I had eight of the same kind—two white, two beige, two light pink, two light peach—but he wasn't listening.

"Oh shut up!" his wife had said to him. "Why do you wear the same J. Crew polo shirt every day? You have twenty, but that's O.K. She wants to be cool and comfortable is why, right?"

"If they're four different colors why do they all look the same?" the boy asked.

"Clorox," I said. Tomatoes and Clorox were two things I hadn't been able to give up for the macrobiotic, biodegradable way of life.

I looked over to the counter where there were several pounds of red tomatoes and a few pink ones.

"These are better," my neighbor said, picking up one of the pink ones. Then she sliced it with a long, sharp, pointy knife.

Her knives were always sharp, I noticed whenever I used one. Our knives were always dull, and I thought about this whenever I read about the woman who had mutilated her husband with a kitchen knife. Such an act would never occur to me, even if I were so inclined, because nothing can be cut that easily with our knives. For several years I've been asking my husband to sharpen them—he has the necessary tools handy but he never does it. This is a good reason to mutilate a man, I would think. The first little touch would wake him, the first sawing motion that gets nowhere, even to slice a tomato. I'd read in a cookbook, "You can severely mutilate excellent tomatoes with a dull knife." "That's for causing me to ruin so many tomatoes with dull knives" could be my defense.

"Taste this," my neighbor said. "Then taste this one, and tell me what you think. I won't tell you which is from which farm, because I know you think one farmer might be an anti-Semite."

"They all are, probably. No, most hate all the summer people, but one blames everything on the few Jews he knows."

"I could kill myself. I bought ten pounds of these and they're lousy and one pound of these and they're fantastic."

"How can they be good when they're so pink?" I asked.

"You can't judge a book by its cover," the boy said.

"Avoid the company of agitated minds. . . . If you are in the presence of people who are excited, angry, and anxious, you will naturally move toward these states." I'd read this in the comprehensive manual of wellness *Natural Health, Natural Medicine,* and I thought of this household as an example of how that worked. This household, and also the personality of Dr. Arnold Loquesto.

I'll taste the tomatoes and leave quickly, I decided. But to my surprise the pink tomato tasted better than the red one. "You're right," I said. I tried to sound calm.

"Now I have to run back and get more before they're sold out!" my neighbor said. "What will I do with this crummy ten pounds? Do you want some?"

"I have my own bad tomatoes. I stopped going to the better farm after they lied to me about flowers and just stopped short of referring to someone as 'a little Jew.' "

"I go to whoever has product," she said. "And I'm half Jewish. You're only one-fourth, or whatever." I'd never heard the word "product" used this way.

"Do you buy Hanro underwear when the label says 'Made in Germany'?" I asked.

"No! Please don't tell me this! It's made in Switzerland! Do you buy it?"

"It must have been one freak pair. When I pointed it out to the store owner, an Orthodox Jew who was wearing a skullcap, he said he'd send them back."

"I can't believe it! Hanro! The best. What will I do with these tomatoes is my immediate crisis. Underpants I can deal with later."

"Take them back and exchange them for corn."

"Their corn isn't as good, either. I only buy corn from the crazy one you won't go to."

"Exchange them for broccoli and cauliflower. They told me they don't spray those. They spray only the corn, if you can believe them."

"I'm not bringing them back. I'll make sauce. Is that a good idea?"

"It will be acid sauce."

"I'll put in sugar, something you would die before you would do. Am I right?"

"Put in carrots and onions. And all the basil from you garden."

"O.K., and then will you come for dinner? Ramona! Ramona, please come and get this sauce started! How many carrots? I'll use sugar because that's what I know. Can I get you a few pounds while I'm there, or do you like to pick out your own?"

"I have to start going there again. I'll pick my way around the crude remarks."

"What else besides the anti-Semitic incident? Where's my housekeeper?"

"Well, they lied to me about snapdragons."

"What kind of lie? Tell me, I must know. Only you would take this to heart. I have a thick skin and can buy produce anywhere on the island."

"I asked for light pink snapdragons and he wrote it on the blackboard with the orders. I left the beach at six the next day to get to the farm—even though I'd just gotten to the beach at five and wanted to stay until seven. His cousin was at the flower stand and he said, 'We don't have any pink.' I said, 'Are you sure? Jim said they'd pick them today.' He said, 'I'm sure, because I'm the one who picked today.' Then the next day I asked Jim when there might be some again. He said, 'Oh, we have them, I just forgot to pick them. Bill made up what he told you. I thought he did a good job with that story, don't you?' "

"You want better produce, so you'll have to steel yourself to go back, right?" my neighbor said.

The housekeeper arrived wearing a white uniform.

"O.K., Ramona. I want to make a very delicious sauce from these lousy tomatoes, so do what this artistic person says and put in all my onions and carrots and basil and if that doesn't work we'll add sugar. What do I care? I have a cupboard filled with candy."

I'd been up for only a few hours and suddenly I was tired. I didn't want to see onions yet. Soon the other members of the household would start coming in for lunch and arguments. Even if they weren't arguing, it sounded as if they were, because they all talked at once. Especially loud were the two teenage boys, who stayed out late at night, then came home with drunken friends who threw up in the wildflower field owned by the conservation foundation. I knew this for a fact, because sometimes I was up listening to a repeat of "Crossfire," and our bedroom was right on the lane next to the field. Then the boys would sleep until one and stumble downstairs to punch one or both of their little brothers. That would start them all yelling. Then into the kitchen to eat cereal and milk in bowls, which they left on the table when they were through. Next, a fight with their mother about where their new polo shirts were. The husband, a Wall Street wizard, would come in talking into his portable phone and start asking where his expensive sports equipment was. The nine-year-old boy was often morose. The five-year-old boy was angry, too, although he had some charm, which came through from time to time. Once he asked me the question "Have you ever tasted dog food?"

"No, what an idea! Why do you ask?"

"Well, I saw someone eat dog food on television and ever since then I've wanted to eat some so badly."

"It wasn't dog food," I said. "They put a label on a can of beans so it would look like dog food."

"No, it *was* dog food! I saw it! It really was!"

The more I explained how these things were done, the angrier he got, and he finally stormed out of the room.

Then one afternoon when I was trying to deadhead some perennials in the border near their property, I heard all four boys fighting. The oldest one did something mean and rough to prevent the nine-year-old from helping with a task they'd all been assigned as if they were a normal American family. It was an activity like gluing something down or putting some water sealant on a piece of wood. A few seconds into the project the fight started. "You little f——," the nine-year-old shouted at his big brother.

"Children, the word is not a noun," I thought I could go over and say, but we weren't on friendly enough terms. And I didn't want to sound like Miss Jean Brodie. "You little f——head!" was something I'd heard children say, and it sounded better.

I was the only person in the neighborhood who was speaking to the family since they had done a number of bad things. They didn't care, or hadn't noticed, how they were treated. If they had things to do over, they would do the exact same things. The worst thing they had done involved picking berries.

In a field near our neighborhood, wild raspberries grew over a fence. It was the custom for children to go by each day and pick whatever they could reach. It was also O.K. to bring a small stepladder or chair to reach a bit higher. No one ever picked more than a cupful. But this family decided they had a way to get more berries, and the way was to drive their Mercedes station wagon next to the field and climb on top of it. The dirt road was so narrow that the gigantic vehicle took up the entire width. When other cars tried to go by, the family kept right on picking. "They picked the brambles clean!" one lady from the D.A.R. would say for years to come. "They left that car there! Can you believe it?" This lady attributed their manners to what she suspected was half of their religion and said, "What did they need all those berries for? Was it to bake their Rosh Sha Hanna pies?" This sounded like something Ezra Pound might have said. Also, intentionally incorrect pronunciation is often a sign of anti-Semitism.

"Are pies part of the holiday?" I asked this woman.

"What else could they need that many berries for?" she said.

I remembered what I'd read in the "Vegetation on the Cape" chapter in the Wallace Nutting book, *Massachusetts Beautiful*:

> As we wound along a by-road we came upon a neat cottage worthy of portrayal. As we skirted about it we discovered the most luscious and wonderful cultivated blackberries we have ever seen. They were at the acme of perfection and we look back to the hour . . . in which we exhibited a marked degree of Christian fortitude. . . . With no one looking, and even the cottage locked and everyone absent, was it not a mark of deep-down religion which prevented our even tasting? How we wanted to try those berries! " 'Twere worth ten years of peaceful life one quart of their array!"

I thought about going home to the kitchen of our rented house. It would be more peaceful there. But I was afraid I'd see my husband coming in from his five-mile jog in the midday sun. You could tell him that the Surgeon General and every medical authority in the world had warned against this time of day for running, and he would keep right on doing it. (Even when the Surgeon General was a respected appointee, unlike the one who told David Letterman her lunch included Campbell's beef soup and a Diet Coke.)

It had taken ten years to get my husband to remove his sweatshirt before running at noon. "I love to sweat," he'd say. Later on, I reminded him, "We have nothing in common."

"We have things in common," he'd said. But I was so surprised to hear it that I forgot to ask, "What?" And I really wanted to know.

If he took a shower first, at least it would be clean sweat. His reasoning was, then he'd have to take two showers in close succession. I'd just read that President Kennedy had had a shower fixation and took dozens of showers a day. Of all the things I'd admired about the President I would have admired that the most, had I known about it earlier in my lifetime infatuation with him and his memory. I haven't recovered yet from watching every documentary shown for the last anniversary in November. It's especially painful to see him and then see Clinton. Just comparison of the two heads of hair is enough to bring about a sense of doom.

I decided to stay in my neighbors' kitchen until I couldn't stand the commotion any longer. That happened when the husband came in with some sports equipment so new and modern that I couldn't even tell what it was. He'd Roller-bladed home from playing tennis and doing another activity involving a newfangled kind of sailing. Pieces of brightly colored equipment from each sport were still on him. A family who'd once tried to buy this house were related to someone in

Eisenhower's cabinet. Their equipment would have been older and more worn.

Members of the family had come into the kitchen and were looking for lunch. The housekeeper was making the tomato sauce while her mistress was slapping sandwiches together. Everyone pulled up chairs the way rustlers and cowhands do in movies. Plates of things were slammed around.

"This could be the best tomato I've ever had," my neighbor said, taking a dainty bite of her sandwich. "Go taste the rest of this one," she ordered me.

I got up and went over to the counter where the sharp knives were kept. I was always glad to get a chance at those knives. Just as I started to slice the remainder of the tomato the husband said, "Why don't I have any tomato on my sandwich?"

"Because you have lobster salad on your sandwich. I have only tomato on mine," his wife said.

"I don't see why that means I can't have tomato on my sandwich."

"Because I have tomatoes, you have lobster. That's the way it goes."

"I can't see why that means I can't have tomatoes. There are dozens on the counter."

"Here," I said, handing him a saucer with the tomato I had just sliced. It seemed like the sensible thing to do.

"Thank you," he said to me as he put the tomato slices on his sandwich. "By the way, would you give your husband tomatoes on his sandwich?"

"If I didn't, it would be just bread and lettuce," I said. "Anyway, I should be going."

"Take a tomato with you," my neighbor said. "And let me know how you do with that farmer."

I crossed the lane onto the parched brown grass of our rented property. It certainly was bleak. A small, new tree seemed to be dying. I turned the hose on and put it at the bottom of the little tree even though it was against the rules to water during a drought. I figured I was entitled to the water because of the extra showers my husband refused to take and also because of all the leftover water resulting from President Kennedy's life being cut short.

It was quiet in the kitchen. It was as hot and still as a room in a book by Carson McCullers. There was nothing I wanted to do.

My husband appeared, clean and dressed. "I couldn't go that far today. My knee is still hurting. I just want a lettuce-and-tomato sandwich."

"Try this," I said, handing him the tomato. "How do people have so much self-confidence?" I said.

"They're farmers. They don't think a lot."

"Not the farmers, the neighbors."

"Oh, them. I don't know," he said. Then in order to make me happy he added, "I wish I did." But I knew he wasn't interested in how people got to be the way they were, not even Dr. Loquesto, whose personality development I asked him to speculate on every week, or every day.

I stepped out onto the porch and looked around. There were no birds or butterflies. It was like a moment from *Silent Spring*.

"Let's go get birdseed," I called into the kitchen.

. . .

The day after the tomatoes, both husbands left for cities. I went to the beach at four o'clock and decided to leave early to get to the farm on time.

I pulled up to the old red truck the farmers used as a stand. When I first met the farmer he was young and now he was not so young, but still looked the same because of his life of constant physical exercise.

"Well, I haven't seen you in a long time," he said in a friendly way.

"We can't get here before seven—that's our problem."

"What are you doing? At the beach all day?"

"No, just from four to seven."

"What do you do before that?"

"Wait for it to cool off."

"What about in the morning?"

"We go bird-watching or on wildflower walks." The truth was I'd never accompanied my husband on his 6 A.M. bird-watches or nature walks, because I stayed up most of the night trying to photograph in the dark. I'd read that Maria Mitchell stayed up all night scanning the sky and making observations. The article didn't tell what time she got up in the morning.

"I thought maybe you were angry about the snapdragons," he said.

"Why would I be angry?" I said. I wanted to skip right over that and feast my eyes upon the vegetables. I picked up a basket of cherry tomatoes and washed a few under the outdoor faucet so I could eat them.

"I ate a pint of those already," the farmer said. "Look at my lip." He showed me a blister. "That's from the acid," he said.

I ate a few more. "Are there any regular tomatoes?" I asked.

He pointed me to a secret place behind some trees. "I was saving those for tomorrow, but you can take some. Let's see," he said, inching around the crate. "How many do you need?"

"Ten or fifteen? How much are they, by the way?"

"How much do you want them to be?"

"That's up to you."

"How's two dollars a pound?"

"Whatever you want." I was ready to pay any price, get some corn, and make a quick exit.

I walked over to the corn stand, where I saw his youngest son, who had suddenly gotten to be sixteen. He had his shirt off, and as I was staring at his chest, along came his uncle.

"Your nephew is all grown up," I said. "You're lucky he turned out to be such a nice boy." I meant it, too, not just about his physique.

"He's a lot better than I was at that age."

"Really? I wouldn't have thought that."

"I was sent to reform school even."

"I can't believe it."

"Well, all I did was, one winter back in Maine we broke into a guy's house. We didn't do much damage, but he was the only Jew in town and the case came up before a judge who was the only other Jew in town."

"What crime did you commit?" I asked. Suddenly I remembered that he was of German descent. It could have been any kind of crime in that case.

"Oh, knocked over a table that broke. It was just for fun."

I was gathering up some corn and squeezing the tips to see if worms had eaten them away. Peeking into corn was forbidden. But since the farmer was distracted by memories of his boyhood pranks I was able to look into a few ears and get all worm-free ones.

"Then I enlisted in the army and got straightened out," he said.

"I never knew you were in the army," I said.

"*Catch-22* is my favorite book," he said.

"I wouldn't have guessed that," I said.

"Usually I like things with sex, but *Catch-22* is the exception."

"It's one of my favorite books, too," I said, backing away.

"I don't read much," he said. "I'd rather watch girls play volleyball."

I started walking backward toward the tomato truck.

"Don't you want some bread?" he said. Then he surprised me by calling, "Man can't live by corn alone."

That night I went across the lane with a supply of tomatoes and corn for my neighbor.

"I can't believe you would do this, you special, unique person!" she said. "And you had no problem with the farmer, right? Here, taste this carrot cake."

"I can't. My stomach is sticking out," I said.

"It is not! How could it be? It's an eighth of an inch out."

"Too many tomatoes. Too yin and watery."

"You could come to my gym—not that you need to."

"I can't stand the music."

"They don't play Mozart at gyms. It has no beat."

"They could play all allegrettos."

"It's just water weight. I can give you some of my diuretic."

"I have some herbal diuretic. Actually, it's corn-silk tea," I said.

"You mean if I eat corn silk, it's diuretic?"

"No, pour boiling water over it and drink that. But do you want to get up all night to go to the bathroom?"

"It all depends on how depressed I am about my weight. Let me show you what I got at the health-food store in addition to my prescription diuretic from the drugstore."

She handed me a bottle. It listed juniper, uva-ursi, marshmallow root, ginger root, and cramp bark.

"This isn't exactly a diuretic. It's for PMS," I said.

"I can't believe they sold me this," my neighbor said. "You wouldn't let me give you some harsh chemical diuretic? It works right away. Did you hear what happened today? I'm awakened at 7 A.M. by a loud knock on the door. It's the sheriff or someone, with a document giving me a week to sign the release on the land near our house in Connecticut. I'm sick that I can't have it. And don't tell me I have so much. That hurts me deeply."

"Well, you have these two houses in the most beautiful parts of each town."

"I deserve more. I can have Scalamandré fabric in every room. I deserve whatever I want. My mother brought me up to believe that."

"My mother brought me up to believe the opposite."

"I'm entitled to whatever I want, and I want that land. I demand to see the purchase-and-sale agreement first. 'Where's the P and S, I'd like to know?' I asked their lawyer. My dreams out the window, my husband doing nothing to get me what I want. Why did I marry this man?"

"I wish I had married Prince Charles," I said.

"I wish I had. Isn't he wonderful?"

"Not that wonderful. But at least we have things in common."

"I was available, too. What things?"

"Organic gardening, vegetarianism—hatred of modern architecture. And he paints watercolor landscapes."

I remembered seeing a photograph of the Prince sitting on the Scottish moors with his paintbox. His cheeks were rosy and the cleated soles of his shoes were visible and perfectly clean. I'd read in an antique book, *What England Can Teach Us About Gardening,* "We cannot be a pink-cheeked nation until America is one great garden as England is." All these things came together in a way that made me wish for a life with the Prince.

My neighbor was still reviewing her marriage. "My other boyfriends were successful, too, but they couldn't have helped children with homework. I married him because I care very deeply about the world of ideas. Not that you could tell from my life."

"You read a book this summer."

"I did? What was it? Come look at my carpet before you go. Can you believe they laid this carpet with the print upside-down?"

I followed her into the Scalamandré-filled living room to the stairway. The youngest boy was sitting on the steps, and the dog was sleeping with its head on his lap.

"Can I take a picture of this?" I asked.

"Yes," the boy said.

"We have a thousand pictures. Look at the carpet pattern," his mother said.

"Maybe he'll never sleep this way again," her son said.

"He will, he will. Now, does this look like an upside-down fern frond or does it look geometric and abstract?" I bent down to examine the carpet.

"If you look closely, you can see the fern. If you ran up the steps, you wouldn't know what it was."

"Good, so I shouldn't do it over? Look at it the other way. Go upstairs."

I went upstairs and looked down the staircase. I was beginning to feel dizzy from the heat of the day, which was still trapped in the house. All the windows were closed. I wished I could go across the lane to our house, where all the windows were open and fans were on in all the rooms. "O.K., I see the fern now," I said.

"I should do it over, right?"

"If you want to see the fern."

"Come with me. I have a remnant, but it's more blue."

We walked down the hallway. On the way, I saw that everything matched everything else.

"Do you like the worn look, or the new carpet on the stairs?" she asked as she led me back. "Should I tear it up and get a worn Oriental runner?"

"This will get worn quickly with the children and the dog."

"But can I wait for the worn look? Would it be better to have it instantly? Would you look at this picture frame?"

I looked and saw a gold-leaf frame on an antique sampler. "The plumber dropped this one and it has a crack in the paint. Now look at the matching one. Should I deduct from his bill and get a new one made?"

"No, get him to drop the other one the same way."

"It doesn't bother you?"

"No, it looks like a piece of molding I saw in Florence."

"O.K., now let me unroll this carpet."

We went to her older sons' room. It was all dark green and navy blue. No wonder these boys were always in a bad mood. The room had been neatened up. I didn't see any *Playboy* magazines, but I could feel that they were hidden somewhere. Like a psychic gardener we had the misfortune to have for a while.

"Did you see my sunglasses?" I once asked this gardener.

"I feel they're between two layers of fabric," she said. But they were right out on the kitchen table.

"Your skin is better than mine," she said on another occasion.

"Only because you go in the sun," I said.

"No," she said, "I've had many near-death experiences."

As she drove off in her truck I realized I should have called out, "By the way, what were the near-death experiences?" Instead I called, "What about the buckwheat-hull mulch?"

"I have all my suppliers searching for it," she said in a lying way.

But here in the dark room in Nantucket I kept wondering, Where do they stash the *Playboy*s, even though I didn't want to know. I wanted to get on with the carpet viewing.

"Is the other fern more visible?" my neighbor asked.

I was kneeling on the floor and staring at the tiny fern. I no longer understood the pattern. The white stitch was outside the realm of the green stitch and didn't seem connected to it in any way. Was the gray part of the white, or was the green part of the gray? I couldn't tell.

"I don't understand in what way this is a fern, really," I said.

"You mean, so forget the whole thing and let it look geometric?"

"Now I can't remember what the other one looks like. Can we compare them?"

We left the room with a sample piece of carpet.

When we got to the staircase and put the piece next to the step, neither one looked like a fern anymore.

"I was wrong," I said. "There's hardly any difference."

"What would you do?"

"I don't have carpets. I have old rag rugs."

"I don't have your spirituality or aesthetics. I can't wait and collect things."

We went out the front door onto the steps. "Your roses need to be deadheaded," I said. "Look at how many new blossoms you can have."

"I asked for white and they gave me light pink."

"I like the pink. Maybe I'll clip them for you tomorrow."

I went across the lane to our empty house. The lights were on, but it didn't seem cheerful. What lay ahead for me? David Letterman and "Crossfire" were all I had to look forward to. Maybe I should have stayed and worked on the roses alone in the dark.

I turned around and started to go back. There was almost a full moon shining over the roses. I could see some stars but I couldn't locate the Big Dipper without my husband to point it out. It was just as well, because he'd get me started thinking about infinity and that always brings on a feeling of going insane. Then I stopped. Because on the other hand, why should I ever go back there again? I didn't fit in with family life. There had to be other places I could go instead. The house and observatory of Maria Mitchell, the first woman astronomer, were only a few blocks away. I remembered seeing the tiny nineteenth-century dress the astronomer wore as an infant. In her room was some lavender-blue wallpaper with little stars on it.

Was it the original wallpaper? Nobody knew when I inquired. But how much could I learn from studying the Maria Mitchell birthplace and observatory? Maria and her descendants were no longer around. No tomatoes were being eaten there. Probably tomatoes were still thought to be inedible in the heyday of the first woman astronomer.

For twenty years I'd been trying to get down the road to revisit Maria Mitchell's house. I'd read that one night in October of 1847, when the astronomer was observing stars through a British-made telescope, "she recognized an unusual, bright object moving slowly across the sky." When her father climbed to the roof he confirmed that she had discovered a comet. "A group calling itself Women of America, exultant over her discovery, gave her a new telescope."

I could give up dealings with other people and confine myself to nightly observations of the sky and the world. Surely my discovery and photographs of Dr. Arnold Loquesto were as important as the discovery of a comet. Why didn't the group Women of America exult in my discovery of the surgeon and give me a new camera, or at least give him a new hysteroscope? A woman did give me the Wallace Nutting book *Massachusetts Beautiful* because she was so grateful that I'd recommended Dr. Loquesto to her. When I told the surgeon, he said, "You should have given it to me." The reason I didn't give it to him was that Massachusetts was no longer as beautiful, and he might feel bad when he saw the photographs in the book.

Things were different when Maria Mitchell lived in Nantucket. I'd read that Thoreau used to come and give lectures—Emerson and Melville, too. I bet they'd never discussed a purchase-and-sale agreement, or heard the nickname for it—the "P and S." And there was no such term as "PMS," either. The other "p" word wasn't bandied about or allowed to be mentioned at all. I'd managed to go my whole life without saying it once.

Maybe that was the time of the world of ideas. But this was the new world. What kind of world was it? It was some other kind of world, and there was no escape.

Who Knows Why

I have to be careful where I go in this town. Because last week I used an obscenity. I actually called out an obscene directive to a clerk in a paint store. I can't believe that I did such a thing.

At the time, I was with the floorman—a friend of ours— and later on he complimented me for having done it. "But there's no excuse for what I did," I said. I was sick with remorse.

"Why? It was appropriate for the situation," he said. "It was perfect, as a matter of fact."

But I always compare myself to Jacqueline Kennedy whenever my behavior falls short of my expectations, and I know that she would never under any circumstances have used a curse word in public. I make the comparison even though I'm a generation below hers, to say nothing of my social class; I'm closer to her daughter's generation than to hers, but I know that her daughter would never use the word, either. Although I did see Princess Radziwill in an organic-food market one June day, and when the item she was searching for was unavailable she said, "Blast it!" I'd never heard the words exclaimed before, or even said in the U.S.A. I had followed the Princess down the street in East Hampton, not on purpose, just coincidentally; we were on the way to the same store.

First, I'd noticed the Princess in another food store without knowing who she was. She was headed toward the freezer. The reason I noticed her was that she had perfect-looking legs and arms. Her limbs were visible because it was the beginning of a heat wave and she was wearing khaki shorts and a white silk T-shirt. She walked over to the freezer in a floppy but determined way. Her hair was wet, and the back section was pinned up to her head with a clip, the way my hair might be during a heat wave. I thought she was just some forty-four-year-old woman I'd never seen in these parts before. But when I checked to see what face went with the perfect limbs I was surprised to recognize Princess Radziwill. She wasn't wearing any makeup on her extremely young-looking face.

As the Princess gathered up some ordinary-looking peaches and nectarines, I stared at her and calculated her waist to be about seventeen inches—almost the same size as Scarlett O'Hara's and also the same as a neck measurement I'd seen in the collar of a shirt owned by Dr. Arnold Loquesto, the world-renowned reproductive surgeon I'd consulted and later photographed.

Eventually, I left the store for the street, where the temperature was on its way up to a hundred, although it wasn't even 10 A.M., and before I knew it the Princess was in front of me, walking in her fast, unique way to a little sports car. She opened the door and dropped her bag of groceries inside, then walked quickly down the street and into the organic store. I must admit, I did want to know which organic product the Princess would be interested in. I hoped she wouldn't be buying any juice from the juice bar, because I had studied the setup at this place and the hygienic situation was not good. The carrots were none too clean, in my opinion. There wasn't much else to buy there. There was only one of everything, or not even one—there was one of a few things. There were no prices. When you inquired about a price, all the sales help would fall into a dither asking each other, and then start guessing. If anyone asked for produce, they'd say, "In the cooler." Once the owner did a little pirouette and said, "Come with me into the cooler!" The cooler, I saw when he opened the door, was at least clean. In the early days of organic food, customers were expected to go into unclean coolers all the time and pick their carrots out of big plastic sacks on the floor. But I didn't want to dwell on that part of my life, the hours spent in coolers in lower Manhattan digging out carrots.

I was wishing I could know which item the Princess couldn't find that hot morning when I spied my exercise teacher, wearing a pink tutu. It was actually some kind of tiny summer dress with a ruffled skirt the length of short shorts. Although my teacher is not yet thirty and her legs have excellent tone from her life of exercise, my legs are better shaped and I would never have worn such a getup, unless I was eight years old. Also, this teacher is German and the Germans aren't entitled to dress frivolously. She has a guilty way about her, although she probably hasn't been educated on the subject of what she should be guilty about. She was furtively ordering some kind of strange juice combination, like parsley-beet-celery. She had told me some time ago that she would be away this week. So, here at the juice area, I said, "When are you leaving?" and she said, "Right now," most likely a lie she had invented on the spot. She was always hiding something. Everything was a secret. And that accent got on my nerves. "Visualize something," she would say with her eyes closed during the class, so I'd visualize her parents and her grandparents and what they were doing in 1942. "Visualize a mountain or a lake"—she would say—"waves, wind, water—when you do this exercise," but I couldn't. I'd stare right at her—she didn't even look German, with her black pixie haircut; I looked more German than she did—and I'd picture her relatives in their uniforms. I think she knew it, too. That's why she was nervous. She was always trying to cancel my classes for one reason or another—a course in a faraway state, a yoga festival, this or that—and there she was, on a day she was supposed to be going on a trip to Canada, right here in town, having canceled class, and ordering juice. How could I have gotten myself a German exercise teacher? She was the only one who stayed all winter and wanted to have a year-round clientele. That's what she said—who knew the real reason?

I had picked up the "who knows?" line of thinking from many hours of talking on the phone to Dr. Loquesto's thirteen-year-old son. He'd launch into long descriptions of a person or an event, and in the middle he'd say, "Who knows why?"

One incident involved a woman who arrived at his house on a Sunday afternoon with "thirty cakes in three large white shopping bags." It turned out that the woman brought the cakes because she was grateful to the boy for once giving her sixteen different phone numbers where Dr. Loquesto might be reached.

"She's a dentist, and a baker on the side, or else she's a baker, and a dentist on the side—who knows which?—and she keeps experimenting with recipes. Each one is worse than the last. Like one was a carrot cake, but with zucchini, pumpkins, kiwis—it was filled with every vegetable ever farmed! And she always includes a coffee cake with millions of raisins, and *nuts,* which I hate. Then, one was a plain yellow cake with a spongelike feel. When you cut into it with your fork, water would pour out."

"It must have been rum," I said.

"No, I swear to you it was *water,* believe me, plain *water!*"

The dentist-baker and her husband and two little children stood on the lawn for a few minutes with the thirty cakes in the three bags. They put the bags down and began discussing different routes they had taken to get to Massachusetts from Rhode Island. Then they left.

"People do that—they go for drives in good weather and discuss the roads they took," the boy explained.

Although he noticed these kinds of things, he was able to lead a normal life and knew how to use a computer.

I had child-sat and cooked vegetarian dinners for him a few times, but he never ate any of the meals. The surgeon himself wouldn't eat a mixed-leaf salad I'd brought to a dinner, saying, "I eat only light green, not dark green." Probably the boy described my salads the way he described the dentist's cakes: "She arrives with twelve kinds of lettuce, and washes the leaves hundreds of times and asks for a lettuce spinner—which we don't have—while talking about the waste of paper towels, and ecology, and who knows what other liberal ideas. The salad always has to have this olive-tasting olive oil from some part of Italy—who knows which. I can't eat one leaf of it!"

My only goal that hot June morning was to go to the hardware store and purchase as many fans as I could for the heat wave. But now I was wondering how the Princess could look so good and calmly go about her errands when someone had spitefully built a gigantic concrete house in the style of an airplane hangar right next to hers, with a concrete wall that blocks the view the Princess once had of the sunset, the sky, the beach, and the water. What did she say when that happened? I hoped she used a curse word. Often, I was stopped by strangers on my walks to photograph the nearby pond and they'd ask, "How did the town allow this?"—something I hadn't bothered to research, because I was always wishing we could move away to a normal place where there were no princesses.

But if we moved to a new town I'd need the services of the floorman, and that might start things up again.

All we did was add two small rooms. I haven't even mentioned the builder. That's because he's become the unmentionable one. "Sure, he's the best painter, but is it worth it?" the builder would say about the painter. Then I asked him who he would recommend, and he said, "No one. They've all breathed too many fumes and it's affected them this way."

I'd go into one of the three paint stores and the owner would say "How are you doing with your painter?" and then he'd laugh—a crazed, knowing laugh. Once, this encouraged me to confide in him: "The assistant rolled the paint onto the floor instead of using a brush and it left roller marks all over, so the head painter had to do it again. He took my boxes and files of photographs, and all my camera equipment from my new workroom, and piled it up in the bathtub on top of the boxes. Then he threw in whatever cleaning equipment was around—a mop, a pail, a can of Comet, and a sponge—and sanded the paint off the floor without covering anything. When he finished, everything was covered with light-green paint dust and I couldn't get to my equipment in the tub because he'd repainted the floor and it was wet."

"That sounds like him," the paint-store owner said.

"Do you know any other painters?" I asked.

"I know some good ones, but you have the best. He's a perfectionist. That's the whole thing."

I'd once seen the painter eating a peanut-butter sandwich and a banana in our hallway. "That was Elvis Presley's favorite meal," I said.

"Yeah, but he ate them together on the same sandwich," he said. I was impressed that the painter knew such a thing.

Then I tried asking him for a floorman and he said, "There are two. One drinks. The other doesn't show up."

All the workmen hated each other. They blamed each other for whatever went wrong. The builder fired our plumber and hired his own. One day this new plumber didn't show up— the reason given was that a shark bit his arm and he needed seventeen stitches, or seventeen inches of stitches. When you live near the ocean, you hear excuses of this kind. In the country you hear about hunting accidents, but people never return from those. In the beginning, the builder and the shark-bitten plumber got along—that was before the big bite—then an assistant plumber took over and he made mistakes. The builder blamed it all on our original plumber, the one who never showed up because he had an important job putting plumbing into a new hotel. Later on, when I read a review of the hotel, the only thing that got a good report was the water pressure. I was happy. That's our plumber, I thought, until I remembered that *was* our plumber. Who knew if he'd return after the builder was rude to him?

I trace the cause of the obscenity back to the origin of my acquaintance with the floorman. We were so young at the time that we thought we could have any old floorman do the floors of our apartment in a hundred-year-old building in SoHo. When it came to choosing the stain, the man had only three, and they were all dark brown. Then I noticed the alcohol fumes, and they were coming from him, not from the bucket of floor stain. I also noticed that he had sanded away so much wood that the floor was lower on one side of the room than on the other.

"I love wood," the new, highly recommended floorman said as he got down on the floor and explained how he'd fix the butchering of it. I believed he did love wood, the way he crawled around touching the floor with real feeling.

One thing he did wrong was to ask for old sheets because he forgot to bring drop cloths to keep the sawdust out of the other rooms. But we hadn't been married long enough to have old things, so he went and took a new one from the linen closet.

The other thing he did was to take a piece of a chocolate cake that I had baked. This was before my conversion to macrobiotics. "Homemade chocolate cake is my favorite," he said.

When I recently reminded him of the incident, he said, "Those were my wild days—my drinking days. I believed the refrigerator came with the job."

It didn't occur to me at the time that he was drunk. He was only thirty-one, about eight years older than I was. He had bright-red hair, as bright as Victoria Page had in *The Red Shoes,* and he had white skin and freckles that went with the hair. But he was gruff. One day I asked him if he was related to a girl I'd known in college, a girl who had red hair and the same last name. "She's my sister," the floorman said without any expression.

It turned out that the floorman had gone to a good college, too. He'd even graduated, but it wasn't something he liked to talk about. He liked to talk about wood. He wanted to tear up the old linoleum in the kitchen and sand the floor underneath it. He said he bet there was a beautiful pine floor under the linoleum. The thing he hadn't counted on was some black tar paper they used to glue down the linoleum. That had to be torn up and sanded off, too. The old black tar paper and glue flew around in tiny bits and stuck everywhere as he sanded.

There was always something he hadn't counted on— something that got him really angry—and he would keep talking about it as he worked on the floor. For example, he hadn't counted on 110 electrical current. "Everything is two-twenty now! How old is this building? One-ten! I didn't count on that!" he'd mutter as he stuck a fork into the fuse box to keep the fuse from blowing when he plugged in his machine. Luckily, I stopped him from using an antique silver fork. We didn't have any spare forks, just as we didn't have any old sheets, and that was how he worked—do you have an old this or that every hour or so, for whatever crisis was coming up. "It won't hurt anything," he'd say, going to the fuse box with a silver fork in hand. He had a Dr.

Frankenstein look as he approached the box: "It's just fork prongs in a fuse." You had to keep your eye on him all the time.

On the last day of the floorman's first job for us, twenty years ago, he arrived for work wearing a heavy tweed suit that must have been from Ireland or Scotland. It was a mixture of beige, green, and a rust color that matched his hair. "I'm going upstate for a wedding after finishing here. I don't want to wrinkle my suit so I thought I'd wear it here and change over to my work clothes, if you don't mind," he said. I didn't mind, because I was sure the floorman had nothing up his sleeve in that department.

Over the years, workmen have had things up their sleeves when they changed clothes in our house. A tile man changed his pants in the dining room and then pretended to be surprised when I walked by. Before going through house renovations—tiling, floor work, painting, masonry, carpentry, landscaping—and reproductive surgery, my looks were intact and workmen found reasons to pull off their pants and put on another pair in front of me.

Time passed for us and the floorman. One day we called to ask him to do another room. He came by, looked around, and then complimented us on caring for the floors. I told him I'd discovered a floor waxer and kept him waxing every year until the time I called and a woman answered, "Jesus loves you." She didn't even say hello first.

Then, catching a glimpse of the hundred-year-old fuse box, the floorman said, "Sweetheart, I can't deal with that one-ten voltage again." But it was O.K. for him to call me sweetheart, because he'd taken to calling my husband sweetheart, too. "I forgot about that. I would've thought they'd changed that over by now!"

"What about the fork?" I said.

"Oh, God, did I do that? It's all coming back to me." Then we both started to laugh, but I knew that he probably hadn't changed and would use cutlery again if he had to. "I don't go sticking forks in fuse boxes anymore, sweetheart," he said. "I'm a bit more professional," he added, as if he were going to tip his hat and dance a jig.

After that he moved to Georgia. There was a lot of restoration going on around there. His old clients would call him from all over the country. If the floor couldn't wait for him, he'd tell how to interview other floormen, to see whether they had respect for wood. Our floorman was as sought after as Dr. Loquesto, but he hadn't learned to manage his time the way the surgeon had, so he'd sigh and give long explanations about tung oil, whereas the surgeon would just hang up.

It was when we bought our house that we got the floorman to come up from Georgia for the first time. And it was on that trip that he told us about his recovery from alcoholism. But his recovery didn't help his work. Something always went wrong right away. This time he had to rent a generator from a motorcycle dealer on the highway. I went with him in his van, because even with the recovery from alcohol he didn't have a credit card. He'd rigged up a makeshift seat belt because the van was so old it didn't have any. As I was trying to hook it up, I saw an old apple core on the floor.

"Usually I don't take the lady of the house in my van to get a generator," he said when I pointed it out.

They were curious about us at the motorcycle shop. I was wearing a Liberty of London dress with a faded blue chef's apron over it. I couldn't find the belt and thought the apron would make the dress seem less like a nightgown. The floorman wore khaki shorts and a blue-green T-shirt, but he had a wild look on his face, similar to something I'd seen in photographs of Van Gogh and Ezra Pound.

After a while I got used to having the floorman around. When he asked for an old sheet, I gave him the one he'd ruined fifteen years before. "I'd never get that color on it now—I've invented my own line of tung-oil stain," he said, staring at the color.

When he got around to hand-sanding the stair treads I noticed how well he blended in with the walls and the wood. His skin was the same pale peach as the paint, and his hair was light red—not as red as when he'd done our first floors. His hands were pickled peach, with gold stain deep in the cracked skin of the fingers, and he was tinted from head to toe with sawdust and orange-gold tung oil. A little statue of him would have looked good on the steps.

When the time came to view the samples he'd mixed for the floor, I chose the first one. This thrilled the floorman. "You've reached the highest level of Zen," he said. "Because all it is is plain tung oil on wood. I mixed color into the others, but you chose the purest one. Sweetheart, you understand wood."

After that job ended, I was afraid to see the floorman again. I know that people in later stages of life have been killed off by house renovations, and I was afraid that the floor job and all the work on the house had polished off the remainder of my youthful appearance.

But then he surprised me by passing through our town on a social call with his new girlfriend, who was about forty-seven. I had to admire him for choosing someone near his own age. Lucky for her she had bone structure to hold up the disillusionment and misery that tried to work on her face. She also had manicured nails with red nail polish, and she wore gold jewelry on her fingers and wrists—just the right amount. On her dainty feet she had velvet ballet slippers to go with her black velvet toreador pants. How this lovely lady had ended up with the floorman and his rough, floorlike ways was something I wondered the minute I saw her. The floor-man was dressed up in a blue-striped shirt, a navy-blue blazer, gray flannel slacks, and even those black loafers with tassels. Maybe the shoes were her influence.

We sat down for a drink as if we were four normal people. Our beverages were alcohol-free. I was looking at those painted nails and the small tinkling charm bracelet and won-dering whether I should try out such a look. I remembered reading that nail polish prevents the nails from breathing.

The floorman wasn't in his floor mode, but we persuaded him to get up from the couch and go look at a big black streak on the kitchen floor. In his dark dress-up clothes he no longer went with the colors of the room, and when he left it was a relief.

"What could have eaten through the finish?" he asked a few times when he returned. Then he said, "The entire floor has to be redone." He'd have to put the job together with some other jobs in the vicinity. He was always putting together a few jobs in one area, but usually none of them materialized.

A year went by. I looked at the streak every day. Then the new rooms were in progress and I got an idea. The idea was to build a little potting area in one of the rooms. This had been on my mind since I watched Myrna Loy describe a little flower room she wanted in the movie *Mr. Blandings Builds His Dream House.* I like to watch this movie over and over because it's unrealistic.

Unlike Mrs. Blandings, I didn't tell the builder that I wanted a nice dry stone floor "where it might be wet with flowers and things." All I said was, "Maybe we should have this part of the floor done in concrete or something so I can get potting soil and water spilled on it." If only I hadn't said that and the whole floor had been done in wood. To tell the truth, when I was standing there with my husband and the builder, I did say, "What about a drain?" But I was quickly shouted down: "Pipes under the floor . . . dollars . . . plumbers crawl underneath . . . attach to . . . tear out . . . put in new . . ." Then I said, "What about Mrs. Blandings' little flower sink?"

"Prices were lower in 1948," my husband said really fast. While the builder started to tell how much every single thing he knew about had cost in the forties compared with now, I wandered off. My husband stuck around and listened to the old prices for nails.

Eventually, it got to be the time for the floorman to return. The floors of the new rooms plus the kitchen floor added up to a job worth his traveling time.

The aroma of tung oil and sawdust makes it seem that something good is happening, but I was dreading the moment the floorman would start working in the kitchen. He'd be underfoot again with all his electrical problems, which I knew would crop up.

"It's a good thing you left half the floor concrete," he said after he'd piled the appliances onto it, "because otherwise all this would be sitting out in the rain." Then he laughed.

"But now I have to find the right blue-green to paint it," I said.

He was bent over, hand-sanding a corner, and he couldn't hear because he'd put cotton in his ears to block out the noise of the machine.

"Maybe I should give up and try spatter paint," I said as he unstuffed his ears.

"Spatter paint's for idiots," he said. "You'll see—we'll go to the paint store, we'll pick out the right green."

But since I'd been trained by a watercolor landscape painter to mix peach-tinted off-whites, I thought I could find the right color on my own. I was filled with hope as I entered the paint store. If not hope, then optimism, or just stupidity. I walked through the doorway and caught a glimpse of hundreds of paint chips. When the owner saw me he began to sing "Earth Angel." This had been his custom ever since the time we tried to get the color of moss growing on earth.

After I explained my project, he gave me the bad news: in order to paint a floor, you had to use floor paint. "Sorry to disappoint you," he said. "Only two greens. Of course, we can fiddle around with the formula."

I remembered watching with admiration the way Ralph Lauren had the window frames of the Rhinelander Mansion painted three times until they got the right color. I wanted to write a letter of approval, but I knew that Ralph Lauren wouldn't care what I thought of his paint choices. My published photographs demonstrating how to remove the polo player from various garments hadn't had any impact on the man or his business. I have to face it—compared with Ralph Lauren, I'm no one. Calvin Klein, too. Although I did recently see Mr. Klein walk into a florist's shop in East Hampton and ask for branches. "Do you have any branches?" I heard a voice say in a New York accent, and turned to see a man in shorts and a T-shirt with a sweater tied around his waist. The florist said no, and the designer left. Had she known the man's identity, surely some branches would have been cut down immediately.

Days passed. I went back and forth with sample quarts of paint. The floorman was readying himself to come into the house to work on the kitchen floor. I was worried. I saw him preparing to move everything out of the kitchen into the dining room. He told me his plan: an orderly progression of chairs, tables, and kitchen equipment all placed in a way that would allow us to get to the stove and the refrigerator. On the last day, he'd move the refrigerator out. And I believed him. Never could I have imagined a room piled with tables, chairs, desks, teakettles, boxes of tea, gold coffee filters, crusts of toast, fruit, steel wool, tung oil, paint samples on shirt cardboards, a tape of the *Trout* Quintet, *The Selected Works of Thoreau,* floor-sanding machines, floorman's work clothes, stained work boots, and dress-up moccasins—all in the same spot.

It was a bleak November day when the floorman and I finally set off in separate vehicles for the paint store.

"I'll make my own color if I have to," he said when we got there. "I know how to make green. You start with red." This was news to me. It was frightening news.

"If blue and yellow make green, and red and yellow make orange, you add the orange by starting with red," he said.

"Why are we adding orange?" I asked.

"You want to warm it up, rather than cool it down, you said—didn't you say that?" The floorman was getting a tone in his voice that Dr. Loquesto has right before a tantrum. A patient once told me, "He flew into a rage and knocked over the Betadine and the lamp. Then he stormed out."

I pictured the orange color of the Betadine. That would be right for warming up the green. But I knew the floorman wasn't in the mood for any medical anecdotes so I just said, "Oh." Knowing when to say nothing is important. And I haven't learned that. Although I feel ready to take a vow of silence and enter a monastery. Most likely, women are banned from being monks. I pictured the monkery with all that peace and silence, and monks walking slowly through the greenery. Who landscaped for the lucky monks? If a landscape worker planted a viburnum right against a holly and smashed a little quince in between, and ran off, what would the monks say? How could they keep their vows of silence then? Maybe monks planted their own shrubs. That had to be part of a life of peace and meditation.

I watched the floorman go over to a bunch of crazy-looking colors. His hair was hardly red anymore. It was faded, with some white mixed in, and he was stooped and bent like a man who's been around a lot of trouble for a long time. I'd heard parts of the business calls he had to make each day to arrange his next jobs, his tung-oil company affairs, and also his sympathy calls to his clients who were undergoing house restorations: "It's hell . . . sweetheart, you don't have to tell me . . . deadly . . . the lowest creatures on earth . . ."

And now he'd put it all aside to help me find the right green. But I'd spent the morning trying to find my boxes of twig tea amid the jumble of floor supplies—he'd left a floor-sanding machine in front of the table and I'd been squeezing in between them for two days. "How can you live this way?" I asked him now and then. "What should I do—drink a quart of tung oil? I'm probably immune to the polymerized resins by now and it wouldn't even kill me."

We came up with a simple formula to add to the base. But the accommodating, song-singing owner wasn't behind the counter that day. A serious-looking woman I'd never seen was there this time. And when we told her our request, she said, "Why don't you just pick a color from the chart?"

I heard the floorman sigh.

I explained, "We've tried that. We need to do it this way." I said that the owner did it all the time.

"You can't add color to floor paint or it gets too soft," she said. "We won't be responsible if it wears off."

I explained that it was a tiny piece of floor in a potting area—they wouldn't be held responsible even if it wore off in one day. "It's not even a wood floor," I said. "It's cement."

"Concrete, it's just concrete. Here, let me see the formula book," the floorman said in his gruff voice as he reached for the book.

"I'm telling you right now, we won't be responsible, I don't care who mixed what for you when," the clerk said. "What color do you want? They make enough colors that anyone should find one without making up formulas. That's the job of the paint company. You think you can do better than Benjamin Moore?"

I knew I could do better than Benjamin Moore. Who was Benjamin Moore, anyway? Was he an actual person, like Colonel Sanders, Orville Redenbacher, or Tom Carvel? I'd always pictured him as Thomas Jefferson. I said to the floor-man, "Oh, never mind. Let's go."

"O.K.," he said. "You go on. I want to look at what kinds of junk they sell as sealants." He said this quietly, just to me.

Actually, there was no one in the large paint-can-filled room but the three of us.

"Have you looked at the floor paints?" the clerk asked.

"O.K., I'm leaving," I said to no one, just a general sentence into the air.

When I reached the end of the aisle near the door, I heard the clerk say, "How rude!"

And since my hand was almost on the door handle, about to pull it toward me as I had so many times before—those times filled with hope and anticipation of seeing the right green, but this time empty-handed into the damp gray afternoon, back to the mad tableau the floorman had created in our house—I felt a need to say something. And then I heard the words "F—— you" as I went through the door. The words came right from where I was standing. I couldn't believe it. But I was so far from the counter that they might not have heard. On the other hand, the store was empty. Their AM radio music wasn't on the way it is when unkempt guys are in back, manning the counter. Maybe it sounded like "Thank you." If reprimanded—or arrested, even—for saying the words, I could explain, "I said 'Thank you.' She misunderstood."

Sure, that might work. Because once I heard my husband say "Thank you" to a toll-booth attendant and it sounded just like the other phrase.

What defense could I use? I didn't have Tourette's syndrome. People with that affliction can't control what they're saying. Different defenses flipped through my mind: "Temporary insanity." "Irresistible impulse." "Crime of passion."

By the time I got home, I was deep into remorse. When the floorman came in I pretended that nothing had happened. But he started saying how great it was: "More people should do it," and "You'll get some respect now." I mentioned something about Jacqueline Kennedy, although I felt unfit even to say her name.

When he finished work he suggested we go out for some dinner, but I said I wasn't hungry. I figured I'd never be hungry again. It would go with the life of silence and abstinence I was planning.

That night I tried lying on the couch and watching CNN for a few hours. But I noticed that the floorman had left his sanding machine in the living room. I got up and opened the door to the screen porch. I didn't know whether exposure to the elements might harm the machine. Rain wasn't predicted. Not enough to blow in through the screens, anyway. I grabbed the handles and started to wheel the machine out the door. It was even heavier than I'd suspected. That must have been how the floorman got his stooped-over look.

In order to fall asleep, I drank some tincture of valerian root and tried to do a breathing-relaxation exercise I'd read about in the book *Natural Health, Natural Medicine.* Then I looked through an antique landscaping book and saw a photograph captioned "An Incorrect Base Planting: A popular practice has been the use of a miscellaneous assortment of evergreens in beds close to the house." The sight of the hideously incorrect planting quickly undid the relaxation.

When the kitchen floor dried the next day, all that remained to be done was to get the furniture and the refrigerator moved back in. The floorman had arranged for the builder to come around and give him a hand with that. I was upstairs at the time. What was I doing that was so important that I couldn't have supervised this final moment? "Why doesn't the refrigerator have wheels?" he'd asked when they moved it out of the kitchen. "Because the model with wheels had a brown plastic drawer with the words 'Meat and Snacks' on it," I said.

"Hell, we could have sanded that off!" the floorman said. "You painted out Giorgio Armani's name on the sidepiece of your sunglass frames."

When I came downstairs to look at the floor—it was a beautiful golden red, with everything back in place—I noticed something in front of the refrigerator. A kind of long scrape. "What's that?" I asked.

"Oh, I guess we did that when we moved your no-wheels refrigerator," the floorman said. "It's good—it gives the floor some character."

I looked at it closely. It was more like a long gouge mark he'd filled in with some special concoction—tung oil and stain-colored filler, maybe.

"Who helped you move this?" I asked, looking at the appliance.

"Your builder obliged when he came by this morning to get a check from the man of the house."

I tried to imagine the scene and what they said when they saw what they had done. I kept looking down at the floor because I was afraid to look at the floorman's face. I didn't want to see the sadness and regret.

At least the scrape wasn't black, or as bad as the old one. But I was wondering why a man would travel up across all those states with all that equipment in his van—how he could love wood so much and resand a whole floor to remove a scrape and then move a refrigerator and put a brand-new scrape back in.

"It gives the look of an antique, a certain quality of age and richness—don't you think? Sweetheart, it adds beauty to the wood, don't you agree?"

I thought about it for a few seconds. The answer was no. But I didn't say anything. I didn't say a word.

ABOUT THE AUTHOR

JULIE HECHT was born in Manhattan. Her stories have appeared in *The New Yorker* and *Harper's,* and she has won an O. Henry Prize. She lives in East Hampton in the winter and Massachusetts in the summer. She has been writing stories since she was eight years old.

ABOUT THE TYPE

This book was set in Bembo, a typeface based on an old-style Roman face that was used for Cardinal Bembo's tract *De Aetna* in 1495. Bembo was cut by Francisco Griffo in the early sixteenth century. The Lanston Monotype Machine Company of Philadelphia brought the well-proportioned letter forms of Bembo to the United States in the 1930s.